ABRAHAM, ISHMAEL, AND ISAAC

The Patriarchs

Dr. Maxwell Shimba

Shimba Publishing, LLC
Printed in the United States of America

First Printing Edition 2024

TABLE OF CONTENTS

In the sacred texts of the Bible and the Quran, there are stories of individuals whose lives have transcended the boundaries of time and place. Among these, none shine more brightly than the patriarchs: Abraham, Ishmael, and Isaac. Their stories are not merely tales of antiquity, but enduring narratives that have woven the fabric of belief for millions around the world. This book delves into the lives of these remarkable figures, exploring the intricate relationships, the profound promises, and the enduring lessons that emanate from their tales.

Abraham, known as the "father of many nations," stands as a testament to faith, obedience, and the unbreakable bond between man and the divine. His journey from Ur to the Promised Land, his willingness to offer his beloved son as a sacrifice, and his unwavering faith in God's promises have made him a revered figure in Judaism, Christianity, and Islam.

Ishmael, a child born of the struggle and tension between Sarah and Hagar, is often seen as a symbol of resilience and tenacity. His story, as outlined in the Bible and the Quran, reflects the complexities of human relationships and the inherent challenges of living up to divine expectations.

Isaac, the promised heir, is the embodiment of hope and the fulfillment of God's covenant with Abraham. His birth to an elderly Sarah and Abraham's devotion to raising him as the chosen one paint a portrait of faith, patience, and the ultimate blessings that come with unwavering trust.

Through the pages of this book, we will navigate the passages of the Bible and the verses of the Quran, uncovering the profound moments and divine promises that shaped these patriarchs' lives. We will explore the dynamics of their relationships, the rivalries and reconciliations, and the rich tapestry of their legacies.

As we embark on this journey, we invite you to contemplate not only the historical significance of these narratives but also the enduring lessons they hold for our lives today. The stories of Abraham, Ishmael, and Isaac are more than ancient chronicles; they are windows into the human experience, faith, and the intricate workings of divine providence. Their significance reaches beyond religious boundaries and cultural divides, resonating with all who seek wisdom, guidance, and inspiration.

This book is a humble attempt to shed light on the lives of these extraordinary figures, providing insights, reflections, and a deeper understanding of their place in the religious and historical tapestry of humanity. We hope that by journeying through these pages, you will find a renewed appreciation for the enduring legacies of Abraham, Ishmael, and Isaac, and a deeper connection to the faith that unites us all.

DR. MAXWELL SHIMBA

THE ORIGINS AND PARENTS OF ABRAHAM

The Origins of Abraham

Abraham, originally named Abram, is one of the most significant figures in the biblical narrative, revered as the father of many nations. To fully understand his story, it is essential to explore his origins, including his family background, his birthplace, and his early life. This chapter delves into the details of Abraham's parents, his siblings, and the city where his story began.

The Parents of Abraham:

Abraham was born to Terah, his father, and an unnamed mother. Terah was a descendant of Shem, one of Noah's sons, and belonged to a lineage that played a crucial role in the unfolding of God's plan for humanity.

Genesis 11:26-27 (ESV):

"When Terah had lived 70 years, he fathered Abram, Nahor, and Haran. Now these are the generations of Terah. Terah fathered Abram, Nahor, and Haran; and Haran fathered Lot."

Terah's significance extends beyond his role as Abraham's father; he also represents the continuity of the faithful lineage from Noah to Abraham, through which God's promises would be fulfilled.

The City of Ur:

Abraham and his family lived in the city of Ur, an important Sumerian city-state located in ancient Mesopotamia, which is modern-day southern Iraq. Ur was a significant cultural, religious, and economic center, known for its ziggurat and advanced urban development.

Genesis 11:28 (ESV):

"Haran died in the presence of his father Terah in the land of his kindred, in Ur of the Chaldeans."

Ur's polytheistic culture and worship of various deities contrast sharply with Abraham's later monotheistic faith. The call to leave Ur marked the beginning of Abraham's journey toward establishing a new covenant with the one true God.

The Brothers of Abraham:

Abraham had two brothers, Nahor and Haran. Haran, the youngest, died in Ur, leaving behind a son named Lot, who would later play a significant role in Abraham's story.

Genesis 11:29-30 (ESV):

"And Abram and Nahor took wives. The name of Abram's wife was Sarai, and the name of Nahor's wife, Milcah, the daughter of Haran, the father of Milcah and Iscah. Now Sarai was barren; she had no child."

Nahor married Milcah, his niece, and settled in Haran, another significant city in Mesopotamia, which should not be confused with his brother Haran. Abraham's family ties extended through his brothers, shaping the relational dynamics that influenced later events in the narrative.

The Call to Leave Ur:

Terah initially led his family out of Ur, intending to settle in Canaan. However, they stopped and settled in Haran, where Terah eventually died. The journey from Ur to Haran set the stage for God's call to Abraham, urging him to continue the journey to the land that God promised to show him.

Genesis 11:31-32 (ESV):

"Terah took Abram his son and Lot the son of Haran, his grandson, and Sarai his daughter-in-law, his son Abram's wife, and they went forth together from Ur of the Chaldeans to go into the land of Canaan, but when they came to Haran, they settled there. The days of Terah were 205 years, and Terah died in Haran."

God's Call to Abraham:

After Terah's death, God called Abraham to leave Haran and continue to Canaan, promising to make him a great nation and to bless all the families of the earth through him.

This divine call marked the beginning of Abraham's journey of faith and obedience.

Genesis 12:1-3 (ESV):

"Now the Lord said to Abram, 'Go from your country and your kindred and your father's house to the land that I will show you. And I will make of you a great nation, and I will bless you and make your name great so that you will be a blessing. I will bless those who bless you, and him who dishonors you I will curse, and in you all the families of the earth shall be blessed.'"

Accordingly, the origins of Abraham are deeply rooted in his family background, his birthplace in Ur, and the early influences of his father, Terah, and his brothers, Nahor and Haran. The transition from Ur to Haran and then to Canaan marks the beginning of a significant journey that would shape the history of the Israelites and the world. Abraham's story is a testament to faith, obedience, and the unfolding of God's plan through seemingly ordinary beginnings. Reflecting on Abraham's origins helps us appreciate the profound impact of his legacy on the religious and cultural heritage of humanity.

INTRODUCTION

Abraham, Ishmael, and Isaac are pivotal figures in the history of three major monotheistic religions: Judaism, Christianity, and Islam. Their stories are intertwined and foundational to the beliefs of millions of people around the world. These patriarchs are mentioned in the Bible, specifically in the Book of Genesis, and in the Quran. Let's delve into who they were and their intricate relationships, drawing upon relevant Bible verses as references.

Abraham - The Father of Many Nations:

Abraham, originally known as Abram, is a central figure in these religious traditions. He is often referred to as the "father of many nations" due to the promise God made to him in Genesis 17:5: "No longer shall your name be called Abram, but your name shall be Abraham, for I have made you the father of a multitude of nations." Abraham is known for his unwavering faith and obedience to God's call to leave his homeland and journey to the land of Canaan.

Ishmael - The Son of Promise and Struggle:

Ishmael was born to Abraham and his wife Sarah's maidservant, Hagar. His birth came as a result of Sarah's impatience in waiting for God's promise of a son. In Genesis 16:11-12, God told Hagar about Ishmael: "You are now pregnant and you will give birth to a son. You shall name him Ishmael, for the Lord has heard of your misery. He will be a wild donkey of a man; his hand will be against everyone and everyone's hand against him." Ishmael's life reflects the complexities of human relationships and God's plan.

Isaac - The Promised Heir:

Isaac was the miracle child born to Abraham and Sarah, fulfilling God's promise to them. In Genesis 21:1-2, we read, "The Lord visited Sarah as he had said, and the Lord did to Sarah as he had promised. And Sarah conceived and bore Abraham a son in his old age." Isaac's name means "laughter" because Sarah laughed when she heard she would bear a son in her old age. Isaac was the promised heir who would carry on the covenant God made with Abraham.

The Relationships:

The relationships between these three figures are profound. Abraham is the father of both Ishmael and Isaac, and they each hold significant places in the divine plan. The rivalry between Sarah and Hagar, the mothers of Ishmael and

Isaac, is evident in Genesis 21:9: "But Sarah saw that the son whom Hagar the Egyptian had borne to Abraham was mocking." This tension shaped their relationships.

Isaac, as the promised son, inherited the covenant from Abraham, as described in Genesis 17:19: "God said, 'No, but Sarah your wife shall bear you a son, and you shall call his name Isaac. I will establish my covenant with him as an everlasting covenant for his offspring after him.'" Ishmael, although not the chosen heir, was also blessed by God and became the father of twelve princes, according to Genesis 17:20.

These three figures, their stories, and their relationships lay the foundation for a rich tapestry of religious beliefs, symbolizing faith, sacrifice, and the intricate workings of divine providence. Their significance extends far beyond the pages of ancient texts, influencing the spiritual beliefs and practices of countless individuals and communities across the globe.

CHAPTER 1

THE CALL OF ABRAHAM

In the dawn of human history, in the city of Ur, a man named Abram embarked on a journey that would not only change his life but would also reshape the course of human spirituality. Born into a world dominated by polytheism, where multiple gods and idols were venerated, Abram's early life was shrouded in the obscurity of a time when the concept of monotheism was a rare and precious gem amidst a sea of divine images. Yet, even in these turbulent times, a profound spiritual transformation awaited Abram, a transformation that would leave an indelible mark on the history of faith.

Unveiling the enigmatic beginnings of Abraham, the "father of many nations," takes us back to a time of spiritual ambiguity. In the midst of a city teeming with false deities, Abram's life began with the same uncertainty that characterized the world around him. But, as with many pivotal figures in history, his path was about to diverge from the ordinary. It was a path that would lead him into the annals of religious significance.

The story of Abraham's call is, above all, a testament to the power of faith. In response to a divine call that would challenge the very core of his existence, Abram exhibited unwavering commitment. The call to leave behind all that was known and embark on an unpredictable pilgrimage was not one to be taken lightly. It was a call that demanded profound trust in the one true God, and it signified a readiness to set forth into the unknown, no matter the cost.

This call from the divine was not just an ordinary summons; it was a promise of profound consequence. The Lord beckoned Abram to leave behind his homeland and his kindred and journey to the land of Canaan, a place God would show him. In return, God pledged to make of him a great nation, to bless him, and to make his name great so that he would be a blessing to others. The divine call was a divine covenant, a bond between God and a man destined to become the "father of many nations." In these promises, the foundation of an extraordinary legacy was laid, one that would transcend the boundaries of time and culture and continue to shape the course of human spirituality.

Abram, who would later be known as Abraham, is a central figure in the history of monotheistic faiths. His early life, as recorded in biblical and historical accounts, provides a glimpse into the world in which he grew up and the remarkable journey that lay ahead. Born in Ur, a prominent and flourishing city in ancient Mesopotamia, Abram's life was shaped by the rich tapestry of a time when the beliefs and practices of polytheism held sway, and the concept of monotheism was a rare and precious notion amidst a sea of idols and deities.

In the ancient city of Ur, where Abram's journey began, polytheism was the prevailing worldview. The people of Ur worshiped a multitude of gods and goddesses, each with their own domain of influence and significance. Temples adorned the city, and priests played vital roles in the religious and societal life of Ur. It was in this backdrop of religious diversity and spiritual pluralism that Abram's story unfolded.

As the son of Terah, Abram was born into a family that likely adhered to the customary beliefs of Ur. Terah, whose name is recorded in the Bible, is mentioned as the father of Abram in Genesis 11:27: "Now these are the generations of Terah. Terah fathered Abram, Nahor, and

Haran; and Haran fathered Lot." Terah's influence and beliefs must have played a significant role in shaping Abram's early understanding of spirituality.

Yet, despite the pervasive polytheism of his surroundings and the influence of his father, Abram's life was destined for a profound spiritual transformation. It was a transformation that would challenge not only the beliefs of his time but also the very core of his existence. The divine call that would come to him marked the beginning of a journey that would change the course of human spirituality. Abram's early life was characterized by the ordinary, but his faith and willingness to heed the divine call would set him on an extraordinary path.

In the midst of Ur's spiritual obscurity, a glimmer of monotheism emerged within the heart of this tumultuous age. It is in the context of this city and its prevailing beliefs that we find the first threads of Abram's story, threads that would later be woven into the tapestry of faith that continues to inspire countless individuals and communities to this day. Abram's early life in Ur is a testament to the power of faith to transcend the ordinary and embrace the extraordinary, no matter the prevailing norms and challenges. It is a story of a man who would become the "father of many nations" and whose legacy would reach far beyond the boundaries of his time and place.

The pivotal moment in Abram's life came with a divine call of extraordinary significance. It was a call that would transform his life and shape the course of human spirituality. The divine call is vividly captured in the Book of Genesis, specifically in Genesis 12:1-3, where it is written, "Now the Lord said to Abram, 'Go from your country and your kindred and your father's house to the land that I will show you. And I will make of you a great nation, and I will bless you and make your name great so that you will be a blessing.'"

This divine call, delivered directly from the Lord, marked a radical departure from the norm of Abram's time. It was an unequivocal summons to abandon all that was known and familiar: his homeland, his kindred, and even his father's house. God's command was clear and unwavering—Abram was to embark on a journey to an unknown land, a land that God Himself would reveal in due course. This divine directive not only required a physical departure but also a spiritual leap of faith.

At the heart of this call lay a promise of immense consequence. God pledged to make of Abram a great nation, a concept almost inconceivable for a man advanced in years and without a male heir. The divine commitment included blessings beyond measure and the assurance that Abram's name would be renowned. Moreover, the divine promise held a profound purpose—Abram would become a source of blessing to others.

In essence, the divine call was a divine covenant, an unbreakable bond between God and a man destined to become the "father of many nations." This call, with its blend of faith and adventure, symbolized a sacred trust in the one true God. Abram's response to this call would be a testament to his unwavering commitment and his readiness to set forth into the unknown, no matter the cost.

The divine call that Abraham received represents a pivotal moment not only in his life but also in the history of faith. It was an act of profound significance that would echo through the annals of time, inspiring countless individuals to heed the call of the divine and embark on journeys of faith and transformation. The call of Abraham serves as a powerful reminder of the enduring power of faith, obedience, and the profound blessings that come from following the divine path.

God's call to Abram was far from a mere simple request; it was a divine summons carrying immense significance and promise. The Lord's call was, at its core, an extraordinary covenant that beckoned Abram to embark on a journey that would transcend the ordinary and the known.

The divine call, delivered directly from the Lord, was a solemn directive for Abram to leave behind all that was familiar. He was to part from his homeland, separate from his kindred, and even forsake his father's house. This was not a casual or ordinary relocation; it was a profound spiritual and physical departure into the unknown.

The destination of this remarkable journey was the land of Canaan, a place that God pledged to show to Abram. This land, which held the promise of divine blessings, was more than just a geographic location; it was a symbol of the sacred covenant that would bind Abram and his descendants to God for generations to come.

The promise that accompanied this divine call was nothing short of miraculous. God assured Abram that He would make of him a great nation. This was a bold commitment, considering Abram's advanced age and his lack of a male heir at the time. God also promised abundant blessings, both personal and for the broader community. Abram's name was to become renowned, and, most significantly, his descendants were to multiply to the point where they would be as numerous as the stars in the sky.

In essence, God's call to Abram was a pact with profound ramifications. It marked the beginning of a journey that would shape the course of human history and spirituality.

The call was a divine declaration that would echo through the ages, reminding all who encountered it of the enduring power of faith, obedience, and the blessings that flow from following the path set by the divine. The divine call to Abram was a promise of extraordinary significance, setting the stage for a legacy that would extend far beyond his time and place, inspiring generations to come.

Abram's journey from Ur to Canaan was a profound and transformative undertaking driven by his unwavering faith and obedience to the divine call. There were several reasons why he was summoned to embark on this remarkable journey:

1. The Divine Call: The primary reason for Abram's journey was the divine call from God. God's command was clear and unambiguous, instructing Abram to leave his homeland, his kindred, and his father's house and go to the land that God would reveal to him (Genesis 12:1). This call was a pivotal moment in Abram's life, marking the beginning of a sacred covenant and a new direction in his spiritual journey.

2. Fulfillment of the Divine Promise: God's promise to Abram was not limited to blessings alone but also the assurance that his descendants would become a great nation (Genesis 12:2). This promise was a key part of the divine plan,

and for it to be realized, Abram had to make the journey to the land of Canaan.

3. Trust and Obedience: Abram's willingness to heed the divine call showcased his profound trust in the one true God. His obedience was a testament to his faith and commitment to God's plan. He was willing to leave behind everything that was familiar, even his homeland, to follow the path set by the divine.

4. Spiritual Odyssey: Abram's journey to Canaan was not merely a geographical transition but a spiritual odyssey. It symbolized his unwavering trust in the one true God amidst a world filled with polytheism and idol worship. His pilgrimage to Canaan signified a departure from the spiritual norms of his time and a commitment to monotheism.

5. Foundation of a Covenant: This journey laid the foundation for the covenant between God and Abram, a covenant that would define the relationship between the divine and the chosen people. Abram's obedience and trust in this journey set the stage for the enduring legacy of monotheism and the Abrahamic faith.

Abram, along with his wife Sarai and his nephew Lot, embraced the divine call and set out on this arduous journey, leaving the city of Ur and venturing into an unknown land. This journey was more than a physical relocation; it was a pilgrimage that would come to symbolize faith, obedience, and the enduring power of a covenant with the one true God. It was a pivotal chapter in the life of Abram, who would later be known as Abraham, and in the history of monotheistic faiths.

Abram's journey from Ur to Canaan was not without its challenges and uncertainties. As he embarked on this arduous pilgrimage, he encountered a series of trials that tested his faith and resolve. The significance of his obedience and the foundation of the covenant he entered into with God during this journey would echo through generations, becoming a cornerstone of monotheistic faith.

The physical journey itself was fraught with difficulties. Abram, along with his wife Sarai and his nephew Lot, had to navigate the harsh terrain, endure the challenges of long-distance travel, and face the uncertainties of an unfamiliar land. They encountered obstacles and hardships along the way, but their unwavering faith in God's promise kept them moving forward.

One of the most significant challenges Abram faced was the barrenness of his wife Sarai. Despite God's promise of descendants as numerous as the stars, Sarai was unable to conceive. This challenge tested their patience and trust in God's plan, leading to a moment of doubt and a decision that would have lasting consequences—the introduction of Hagar, Sarai's maidservant, into their story.

Abram also had to navigate the political and social landscape of the regions through which he passed. He encountered foreign rulers, like Pharaoh in Egypt, and had to navigate delicate situations to protect his family. These encounters added to the complexity and uncertainty of his journey.

Despite these challenges, Abram's obedience to God's call remained steadfast. His trust in the divine promise was unwavering, and it is this trust that forms the bedrock of his legacy. The covenant he entered into with God was not only a testament to his faith but also a promise that extended beyond his lifetime. It laid the foundation for the relationship between God and the descendants of Abraham, becoming a covenant that would endure through the generations.

The call of Abraham serves as a powerful starting point in the remarkable tapestry of the lives of these patriarchs. It is a story of faith and adventure, of challenges and uncertainties, and of the enduring power of God's promise. Abram's journey from Ur to Canaan was the beginning of a narrative that would shape the course of monotheistic faith and inspire countless generations to come. His unwavering obedience and trust in the divine call serve as a testament to the enduring legacy of Abraham, a man who would become the "father of many nations."

CHAPTER 02

THE PROMISE OF A SON

In the tapestry of Abraham's life, woven with threads of faith and divine call, one of the most pivotal moments is the promise of a son. This chapter unveils the remarkable assurance given by God to Abraham, a promise that seemed impossible due to his old age and Sarah's barrenness. It is a story of unwavering faith, divine intervention, and the birth of Isaac, a child who would play a central role in the fulfillment of God's covenant.

God's Promise to Abraham:

God's promise to Abraham of a son is a testament to the divine plan and the enduring power of faith. As recorded in Genesis 15:4-6, the Lord said to Abram, "This man shall not be your heir; your very own son shall be your heir." God led Abram outside and told him to count the stars, promising that his descendants would be as numerous as those stars in the sky. This divine assurance was a source of hope and a reaffirmation of God's covenant.

Sarah's Laughter:

Sarah, Abram's wife, plays a significant role in this narrative. Despite the divine promise, Sarah, being well beyond her childbearing years, laughed at the notion of bearing a child in Genesis 18:12. This laughter, filled with doubt and incredulity, is a poignant moment in the story, highlighting the human limitations and the miraculous nature of the promise.

The Birth of Isaac:

Despite the laughter and skepticism, God's promise was fulfilled. In Genesis 21:1-2, we read, "The Lord visited Sarah as he had said, and the Lord did to Sarah as he had promised. And Sarah conceived and bore Abraham a son in his old age." The birth of Isaac, whose name means "laughter," is a miraculous event, a testament to the divine intervention in response to faith and the fulfillment of God's covenant.

This chapter explores the profound significance of God's promise to Abraham and the birth of Isaac, a child who would become a key figure in the unfolding narrative of the patriarchs. It is a story that resonates with themes of faith, patience, and the extraordinary workings of the divine plan. The promise of a son not only reaffirms the covenant between God and Abraham but also symbolizes the limitless potential of faith, even in the face of seemingly insurmountable obstacles.

Introduction:

In the tapestry of Abraham's life, woven with threads of faith and divine call, one of the most pivotal moments is the promise of a son. This promise, an integral part of the patriarch's journey, stands as a testament to the enduring power of faith and the profound workings of the divine plan. It is a story that weaves together the threads of unwavering belief, divine intervention, and the birth of Isaac, a child who would play a central role in the fulfillment of God's covenant. This chapter unveils the remarkable assurance given by God to Abraham—a promise that, given his old age and Sarah's barrenness, seemed impossible to fulfill.

The Promise of a Son:

The promise of a son is a key element in the narrative of Abraham, a man chosen by God to be the "father of many nations." This divine assurance, as recorded in Genesis 15:4-6, serves as a foundational moment. The Lord's words to Abram were clear and resounding: "This man shall not be your heir; your very own son shall be your heir." God's promise was accompanied by a visual aid as He led Abram outside and directed him to count the stars, symbolizing the vast number of descendants that would be born through his lineage.

Unwavering Faith and Divine Intervention:

Abraham and Sarah's journey was not without its challenges. Sarah, in particular, bore the weight of her old age and her inability to bear children. Her laughter, as expressed in Genesis 18:12, was laced with doubt and incredulity when she heard of the promise. However, this laughter, once filled with skepticism, would soon transform into the laughter of joy as the divine promise unfolded.

The Birth of Isaac:

Despite the odds and the skepticism, the promise was realized. In Genesis 21:1-2, we read, "The Lord visited Sarah as he had said, and the Lord did to Sarah as he had promised. And Sarah conceived and bore Abraham a son in his old age." The birth of Isaac, whose very name means "laughter," was a miraculous event. It was a testament to divine intervention, a fulfillment of God's covenant, and the embodiment of faith prevailing over human limitations.

This chapter explores the profound significance of God's promise of a son and the birth of Isaac. It signifies the culmination of a divine plan, the reaffirmation of the covenant between God and Abraham, and the limitless potential of faith. The promise of a son is not just a narrative within the story of Abraham; it is a symbol of the extraordinary workings of faith and the unwavering commitment of the divine to fulfill its promises. Isaac's birth stands as a testament to the power of faith and serves as a pivotal moment in the unfolding narrative of the patriarchs.

God's promise to Abraham is a central and enduring aspect of his story. This divine assurance, as recorded in Genesis 15:4-6, reflects the foundational nature of this promise:

Genesis 15:4-6 (ESV):

"And behold, the word of the Lord came to him: 'This man shall not be your heir; your very own son shall be your heir.' And he brought him outside and said, 'Look toward heaven, and number the stars, if you are able to number them.' Then he said to him, 'So shall your offspring be.' And he believed the Lord, and he counted it to him as righteousness."

In this passage, God speaks directly to Abram, reassuring him that his descendants would not come from his servant Eliezer but from his own offspring. The Lord then leads Abram outside and instructs him to look at the multitude of stars in the night sky, emphasizing the vastness of his future descendants. Abram's belief in God's promise is not only an act of faith but is also counted as righteousness, signifying his unwavering trust in the divine plan.

This promise of a son is a pivotal moment in the narrative of Abraham and a reaffirmation of God's covenant with him. It signifies the beginning of a legacy that would extend far beyond his lifetime, one that is central to the faith of many. The divine assurance is a testament to the enduring power of faith and the remarkable workings of God's plan.

Sarah's laughter is a poignant and significant moment in the narrative of Abraham and the promise of a son. It is recorded in Genesis 18:12, a moment that underscores the very human reaction of doubt and incredulity, given her advanced age:

Genesis 18:12 (ESV):

"So Sarah laughed to herself, saying, 'After I am worn out, and my lord is old, shall I have pleasure?'"

In this passage, Sarah, overhearing the divine visitors discussing her future maternity, cannot help but laugh to herself. Her laughter is not one of joy or anticipation but is rather a reaction to the seemingly impossible prospect of bearing a child in her old age. The words she utters reflect her skepticism and awareness of her physical limitations. The description of Sarah as "worn out" and her husband Abraham as "old" highlight the practical difficulties of such a promise.

Sarah's laughter is a testament to the very real and human reactions that individuals have when faced with the extraordinary and the miraculous. It underscores the remarkable nature of the divine promise and the sheer impossibility of it within the scope of human understanding. Yet, as the narrative unfolds, her laughter would soon give way to the laughter of joy and fulfillment, as God's promise was realized through the birth of Isaac, a child who would play a central role in the covenant between God and Abraham. Sarah's laughter, from incredulity to joy, serves as a poignant and relatable aspect of this narrative.

The birth of Isaac is of immense importance within the narrative of Abraham and the broader context of monotheistic faith. Its significance can be summarized as follows:

1. Fulfillment of God's Promise: The birth of Isaac represents the concrete fulfillment of God's promise to Abraham and Sarah. Despite the seemingly insurmountable obstacles, the birth of a son was a miraculous event that reaffirmed the divine covenant. It served as a tangible demonstration of God's faithfulness to His word.

2. Key Figure in the Covenant: Isaac's birth marked the beginning of a lineage that would become central to the fulfillment of God's covenant. He was not just any child but

the child of promise, the one through whom God's covenant blessings would flow. His role was pivotal in ensuring the continuity of God's plan.

3. Renewed Hope and Joy: For Abraham and Sarah, the birth of Isaac brought about a transformation from doubt and incredulity to joy and hope. It symbolized the ability of faith to overcome human limitations. Isaac's name, which means "laughter," reflects the joy and laughter that replaced Sarah's initial laughter of skepticism.

4. Legacy of Faith: Isaac's birth became a testament to the enduring legacy of faith, obedience, and the remarkable workings of God. It serves as a source of inspiration for future generations, demonstrating that the impossible can be made possible through faith in the divine plan.

5. Continuity of Monotheistic Faith: Isaac played a crucial role in the continuity of monotheistic faith. He was the father of Jacob (Israel), who, in turn, became the father of the twelve tribes of Israel. These tribes would play a central role in the development of the Israelite nation and the preservation of monotheism.

In essence, the birth of Isaac is a transformative and pivotal moment in the story of Abraham. It symbolizes the power of faith, the fulfillment of divine promises, and the beginning of a legacy that would shape the course of monotheistic faith for generations to come. The birth of Isaac serves as a poignant reminder of the enduring nature of God's covenant and the limitless potential of faith in the face of the impossible.

The profound significance of God's promise to Abraham and the birth of Isaac is woven into the very fabric of the narrative of the patriarchs. This story resonates with themes that continue to inspire and shape the course of monotheistic faith:

Faith: At its core, this narrative is a testament to the power of faith. The divine promise of a son, despite human limitations, required unwavering belief in God's plan. Abraham's faith counted as righteousness, and Sarah's transformation from skepticism to joy highlight the transformative power of trust in the divine.

Patience: The fulfillment of God's promise did not happen overnight. It required patience and endurance on the part of Abraham and Sarah. Their journey of waiting and hoping underscores the virtue of patience in the context of faith and the unfolding of God's plan.

Extraordinary Workings of the Divine Plan: The birth of Isaac was nothing short of a miracle. It defied the laws of nature and showcased the miraculous nature of God's intervention. It is a reminder that the divine plan often operates beyond human comprehension and capabilities.

Reaffirmation of the Covenant: Isaac's birth reaffirmed the covenant between God and Abraham. It marked the beginning of a lineage through which God's blessings and promises would flow. It symbolized the continuity of the divine plan and the enduring nature of God's covenant.

Limitless Potential of Faith: The birth of Isaac symbolizes the limitless potential of faith. It shows that, with trust in God's plan, the seemingly insurmountable obstacles can be overcome. It encourages believers to hold fast to their faith even in the face of challenges and doubts.

In this narrative, the Promise of a Son is not just a historical account but a profound reflection of the enduring themes of faith and divine intervention. It serves as an inspiration for believers, a reminder of the remarkable workings of the divine plan, and an affirmation of the limitless potential of faith in the face of seemingly impossible circumstances. The birth of Isaac is a pivotal moment in the patriarchs' narrative, embodying the power of faith and the fulfillment of God's promises.

CHAPTER 03

THE BINDING OF ISAAC

The narrative of Abraham and Isaac reaches a pivotal and deeply moving moment in the story of faith and obedience—the binding of Isaac. This chapter explores the profound test of Abraham's faith and the famous story of the near-sacrifice of Isaac. It is a story of unwavering commitment to the divine call, the willingness to make the ultimate sacrifice, and the transformative power of obedience.

The Testing of Abraham's Faith:

The binding of Isaac is a powerful test of Abraham's faith. In Genesis 22:1-2, we read, "After these things God tested Abraham and said to him, 'Abraham!' And he said, 'Here I am.' He said, 'Take your son, your only son Isaac, whom you love, and go to the land of Moriah, and offer him there as a burnt offering on one of the mountains of which I shall tell you.'" This divine command was a monumental challenge, requiring Abraham to offer his beloved son as a sacrifice.

The Near-Sacrifice of Isaac:

Abraham, without hesitation, obeyed the divine command. He journeyed to Mount Moriah with Isaac, where he built an altar and bound his son. However, at the critical moment, an angel of the Lord intervened, preventing the sacrifice. In Genesis 22:12, the angel said, "Do not lay your hand on the boy or do anything to him, for now I know that you fear God, seeing you have not withheld your son, your only son, from me." In place of Isaac, a ram provided by God was offered as a sacrifice.

This chapter delves into the profound significance of the binding of Isaac, exploring themes of faith, obedience, and the ultimate test of one's commitment to the divine. It serves as a remarkable testament to the transformative power of unwavering faith and the blessings that come from following the divine path, even in the face of the most challenging trials. The story of the binding of Isaac remains a poignant and enduring part of the narrative of the patriarchs, a symbol of devotion and the enduring nature of God's covenant.

Introduction:

The narrative of Abraham and Isaac reaches a pivotal and deeply moving moment in the story of faith and obedience—the binding of Isaac. This chapter explores the profound test of Abraham's faith and the famous story of the near-sacrifice of Isaac. It is a story of unwavering commitment to the divine call, the willingness to make the ultimate sacrifice, and the transformative power of obedience.

The Testing of Abraham's Faith:

The binding of Isaac is a powerful test of Abraham's faith. In Genesis 22:1-2, we read, "After these things God tested Abraham and said to him, 'Abraham!' And he said, 'Here I am.' He said, 'Take your son, your only son Isaac, whom you love, and go to the land of Moriah, and offer him there as a burnt offering on one of the mountains of which I shall tell you.'" This divine command was a monumental challenge, requiring Abraham to offer his beloved son as a sacrifice.

The Near-Sacrifice of Isaac:

Abraham, without hesitation, obeyed the divine command. He journeyed to Mount Moriah with Isaac, where he built an altar and bound his son. However, at the critical moment, an angel of the Lord intervened, preventing the sacrifice. In Genesis 22:12, the angel said, "Do not lay your hand on the boy or do anything to him, for now I know that you fear God, seeing you have not withheld your son, your only son, from me." In place of Isaac, a ram provided by God was offered as a sacrifice.

This chapter delves into the profound significance of the binding of Isaac, exploring themes of faith, obedience, and the ultimate test of one's commitment to the divine. It serves as a remarkable testament to the transformative power of unwavering faith and the blessings that come from following the divine path, even in the face of the most challenging trials. The story of the binding of Isaac remains a poignant and enduring part of the narrative of the patriarchs, a symbol of devotion and the enduring nature of God's covenant.

The testing of Abraham's faith, as depicted in the binding of Isaac, is a profound and challenging trial set by God. It is described in Genesis 22:1-2, where God tests Abraham's unwavering commitment to the divine call:

Genesis 22:1-2 (ESV):

"After these things God tested Abraham and said to him, 'Abraham!' And he said, 'Here I am.' He said, 'Take your son, your only son Isaac, whom you love, and go to the land of Moriah, and offer him there as a burnt offering on one of the mountains of which I shall tell you.'"

This divine command represented an extraordinary challenge to Abraham's faith. God instructed him to take his beloved and long-awaited son, Isaac, and offer him as a burnt offering on a designated mountain in the land of Moriah. The command was a test of Abraham's unwavering commitment to the divine call and his willingness to make the ultimate sacrifice, even if it meant offering his cherished son.

The testing of Abraham's faith in this context was a moment of profound trial, one that would reveal the depths of his devotion and trust in God. It was a demonstration of the willingness to follow the divine path, no matter the personal cost or the seeming impossibility of the command. This test of faith would not only be a pivotal moment in Abraham's life but also a testament to the enduring power of obedience and commitment to the divine will.

The near-sacrifice of Isaac holds profound significance in the narrative of Abraham and Isaac, as well as in the broader context of monotheistic faith. Its importance can be summarized as follows:

1. Ultimate Test of Faith: The near-sacrifice of Isaac represents the ultimate test of Abraham's faith and obedience. Abraham's willingness to carry out the divine command to the point of raising the knife over his son was a testament to his

unwavering commitment to God, even in the face of the most agonizing trial.

2. Divine Intervention: At the critical moment, the angel of the Lord intervened, preventing the sacrifice. This divine intervention not only spared Isaac's life but also affirmed God's acceptance of Abraham's willingness to obey. It demonstrated God's compassion and the value of obedience in the divine plan.

3. Symbol of Devotion: The near-sacrifice of Isaac serves as a powerful symbol of devotion and trust in God. It underscores the idea that one's ultimate loyalty should be to the divine, even above the most cherished earthly relationships and possessions. It emphasizes the significance of putting God first in one's life.

4. Foreshadowing: The story of the near-sacrifice of Isaac can be seen as a foreshadowing of Christ's sacrifice on the cross in Christian theology. Just as Isaac was spared from death, Jesus is believed to have been the sacrificial lamb for the redemption of humanity. This narrative carries rich symbolism for Christian interpretations.

5. Continuation of the Covenant: The near-sacrifice of Isaac reaffirms the covenant between God and Abraham. It marks a pivotal moment in the narrative of the patriarchs, highlighting the enduring nature of God's promise and the blessings that come from obedience.

6. Inspiration for Future Generations: The story of the near-sacrifice of Isaac has served as a source of inspiration for generations. It conveys the idea that unwavering faith and obedience can lead to divine blessings, even in the face of the most challenging trials. It encourages believers to prioritize their relationship with God above all else.

In essence, the near-sacrifice of Isaac is a profound and enduring narrative that resonates with themes of faith, obedience, divine intervention, and the transformative power of trust in God. It serves as a powerful testament to the enduring nature of the divine covenant and the willingness of Abraham to make the ultimate sacrifice in the name of faith and devotion.

The binding of Isaac, as a narrative within the broader story of Abraham and the patriarchs, indeed delves into profound themes of faith, obedience, and the ultimate test of one's commitment to the divine. It stands as a remarkable testament to the transformative power of unwavering faith and the blessings that come from following the divine path, even in the face of the most challenging trials. The story of the binding of Isaac remains a poignant and enduring part of the patriarchs' narrative, symbolizing devotion and the enduring nature of God's covenant.

This narrative, at its core, exemplifies the depth of faith and commitment to God. Abraham's unwavering trust in the divine call led him to obey, even when faced with the unimaginable task of sacrificing his beloved son. The binding of Isaac underscores the notion that true faith demands unwavering obedience, no matter how difficult the command may be.

The intervention of the angel of the Lord, preventing the sacrifice and providing a ram as a substitute, emphasizes the compassion and acceptance of God. It reveals that obedience to the divine path, even in the face of profound trials, is met with blessings and affirmation.

The story of the binding of Isaac continues to serve as an enduring source of inspiration for believers. It encourages individuals to prioritize their relationship with the divine above all else, to remain steadfast in faith, and to trust in the transformative power of obedience. It stands as a symbol of devotion and the enduring nature of God's covenant, a narrative that continues to resonate with themes of faith, obedience, and the unwavering commitment to the divine call.

CHAPTER 04

HAGAR AND ISHMAEL

In the tapestry of Abraham's life, there are threads that weave a story of complexity and humanity, and the story of Hagar and Ishmael is one such thread. This chapter delves into the narrative of Hagar, Sarah's maidservant, and the birth and upbringing of Ishmael. It is a tale of family dynamics, faith, and the consequences of human decisions in the context of divine promises.

The Story of Hagar:

Hagar enters the narrative as Sarah's Egyptian maidservant. Her presence is part of the intricate web of relationships in Abraham's household. Hagar's story is one of servitude, but it also becomes a story of hardship, hope, and resilience.

The Birth and Upbringing of Ishmael:

Sarah's inability to conceive led her to take a significant step. As recorded in Genesis 16:2-4, Sarah suggested to Abraham that he take Hagar as a wife to bear a child. Hagar conceived and gave birth to Ishmael. This event raises questions about the dynamics within the household and the consequences of their actions.

This chapter explores the story of Hagar and Ishmael, shedding light on the complexities of human relationships and decisions. It is a narrative that raises questions about faith, obedience, and the consequences of choices within the context of divine promises. Hagar and Ishmael, though often in the background of the patriarchal narrative, play significant roles in shaping the course of history and faith.

Introduction:

In the tapestry of Abraham's life, there are threads that weave a story of complexity and humanity, and the story of Hagar and Ishmael is one such thread. This chapter delves into the narrative of Hagar, Sarah's maidservant, and the birth and upbringing of Ishmael. It is a tale of family dynamics, faith, and the consequences of human decisions in the context of divine promises.

Who Were Hagar and Ishmael?

Hagar was an Egyptian woman who served as a maidservant or handmaiden to Sarah, the wife of Abraham. She played a significant role in the household of Abraham and Sarah. Ishmael was the son born to Hagar, through a union with Abraham. He is considered one of the patriarchs and is an important figure in the lineage of Abraham.

The Nationality of Hagar:

Hagar's nationality is identified as Egyptian. She was an Egyptian woman, and her background likely had an influence on the dynamics within Abraham's household. Hagar's identity as an Egyptian servant adds an additional layer of complexity to the narrative, as it reflects the multicultural nature of the story and the interplay of different cultures and faiths within the patriarchal family.

This chapter delves into the lives of Hagar and Ishmael, providing insights into their roles and contributions to the larger narrative of Abraham and the patriarchs. It explores the intricate relationships, family dynamics, and the consequences of the decisions made in the context of divine promises. Hagar and Ishmael, though sometimes overshadowed by other figures in the story, remain essential characters in the broader tapestry of faith and history.

The story of Hagar is a significant and complex part of the narrative in the Bible. Hagar enters the narrative as

Sarah's Egyptian maidservant, and her story unfolds in several key episodes:

1. Servitude: Hagar's initial role in the household of Abraham and Sarah was that of a maidservant. She served Sarah, Abraham's wife, and was subject to her commands and authority.

2. Barrenness and Surrogacy: Sarah's inability to conceive led to a significant turn of events. In an attempt to fulfill God's promise of descendants for Abraham, Sarah suggested that Hagar become a surrogate mother to bear a child for Abraham. Hagar agreed, and she conceived a son, Ishmael.

3. Conflict and Expulsion: The birth of Ishmael created tension and conflict in the household. Sarah became jealous and mistreated Hagar. Eventually, Hagar fled into the wilderness to escape the mistreatment, and there, she encountered an angel of the Lord who instructed her to return to Sarah.

4. Promise and Hope: The angel of the Lord made a promise to Hagar concerning her son, Ishmael. In Genesis 16:10-12, it was foretold that Ishmael would become the father of a great nation. This promise brought hope to Hagar and Ishmael.

Hagar's story is one of complexity, as it involves servitude, surrogacy, mistreatment, and ultimately a divine promise. She is a symbol of resilience and faith, as she endured hardships and found hope in the midst of adversity. Hagar's role in the biblical narrative is a testament to the interconnectedness of human relationships and the multifaceted nature of faith and family dynamics within the patriarchal story.

The Birth of Ishmael:

The birth of Ishmael is a pivotal event in the biblical narrative, recorded in Genesis 16. It reflects the complexities of human relationships and the consequences of decisions made in the pursuit of divine promises.

Sarah, Abraham's wife, faced a distressing predicament. Despite God's promise of descendants, she remained barren. In her desperation, she suggested a solution rooted in the customs of the time. She proposed to Abraham that he take her maidservant, Hagar, as a second wife to bear a child who could fulfill the divine promise of descendants.

Genesis 16:2-4 (ESV):

"And Sarai said to Abram, 'Behold now, the Lord has prevented me from bearing children. Go in to my servant; it may be that I shall obtain children by her.' And Abram listened to the voice of Sarai. So, after Abram had lived ten years in the land of Canaan, Sarai, Abram's wife, took Hagar the Egyptian, her servant, and gave her to Abram her husband as a wife."

Hagar, as a servant, had little choice in the matter, and the union between her and Abraham was one of obligation. The outcome of this union was the conception of a son, whom they named Ishmael.

The Upbringing of Ishmael:

Ishmael's upbringing occurred within the complex dynamics of Abraham's household. He was born to Hagar, an Egyptian woman, and his birth introduced tensions and conflicts in the family. The Bible does not provide detailed accounts of Ishmael's early years, but it is known that Sarah's jealousy of Hagar and her son became a source of discord.

Hagar and Ishmael faced mistreatment and eventually fled from Sarah's harsh treatment. They found themselves in the wilderness, where they encountered an angel of the Lord.

Genesis 16:7-11 (ESV):

"The angel of the Lord found her by a spring of water in the wilderness, the spring on the way to Shur. And he said, 'Hagar, servant of Sarai, where have you come from, and where are you going?' She said, 'I am fleeing from my mistress Sarai.' The angel of the Lord said to her, 'Return to your mistress and submit to her.' The angel of the Lord also said to her, 'I will surely multiply your offspring so that they cannot be numbered for multitude.'"

The angel's message contained a divine promise concerning Ishmael's future. He foretold that Ishmael would become the father of a great nation. This promise brought hope to Hagar and her son, despite their hardships.

The story of Ishmael's birth and upbringing is a testament to the complexities of human decisions and relationships in the context of divine promises. It highlights the challenges and tensions that can arise from such decisions and underscores the transformative power of divine promises, even in the face of adversity. Ishmael's legacy as a father of a great nation would play a significant role in biblical history and in the broader tapestry of faith.

The story of Hagar and Ishmael, as explored in this chapter, sheds light on the complexities of human relationships and the consequences of decisions made within the context of divine promises. This narrative raises fundamental questions about faith, obedience, and the intricate interplay of human choices within the broader patriarchal story.

Hagar, as Sarah's maidservant, found herself in a position of servitude and obligation within Abraham's household. Her role in the narrative is emblematic of the multifaceted dynamics within the family. The decision to have Hagar bear a child for Sarah, while a cultural custom of the time, led to complexities that would affect the family's dynamics and relationships.

The birth of Ishmael and his upbringing within this intricate context introduced tensions and conflicts, illustrating the human consequences of decisions made in pursuit of divine promises. The jealousy and mistreatment Hagar and Ishmael faced in the household culminated in their flight into the wilderness.

However, the narrative also highlights the transformative power of divine intervention. The encounter with the angel of the Lord in the wilderness brought a divine promise concerning Ishmael's future. Despite the hardships they faced, this promise provided hope and purpose.

Hagar and Ishmael, often in the background of the patriarchal narrative, played significant roles in shaping the course of history and faith. Ishmael's legacy as the father of a great nation and the complexities of his relationship with Isaac, Abraham's other son, further exemplify the intricate connections between these characters and the broader story of faith.

The story of Hagar and Ishmael serves as a reminder that the pursuit of divine promises can involve complex human decisions and relationships. It underscores the enduring themes of faith, obedience, and the profound impact of divine intervention within the tapestry of the patriarchal narrative.

CHAPTER 05

THE COVENANT WITH GOD

The covenant between God and Abraham is a fundamental and enduring aspect of the biblical narrative. This chapter delves into the nature of the covenant, exploring the promises made by God to Abraham and the sign of the covenant—circumcision. It is a story of divine commitment, faith, and the enduring nature of God's promises.

God's Covenant with Abraham:

The covenant between God and Abraham is introduced in Genesis 15. God made a promise to Abraham that his descendants would be as numerous as the stars, and He pledged to give them the land of Canaan. This covenant reaffirmed God's relationship with Abraham and marked a significant turning point in the patriarchal narrative.

Circumcision as a Sign of the Covenant:

One of the distinctive features of the covenant was the practice of circumcision. Circumcision served as a physical sign of the covenant between God and Abraham's descendants. It was a symbol of their commitment to God and His promises.

This chapter explores the profound significance of the covenant between God and Abraham, emphasizing themes of faith, commitment, and the enduring nature of God's promises. The practice of circumcision, as a sign of the covenant, plays a central role in the identity and faith of Abraham's descendants, and it remains a pivotal part of the patriarchal narrative.

Introduction:

The covenant between God and Abraham is a fundamental and enduring aspect of the biblical narrative. This chapter explores the nature of the covenant, delving into the promises made by God to Abraham and the practice of circumcision as a sign of the covenant. It is a story that underscores divine commitment, faith, and the lasting nature of God's promises.

The Imperative of Abraham's Covenant with God:

Abraham's covenant with God is of paramount importance in the biblical narrative and the history of faith. It marks a foundational moment in the relationship between God and humanity. The covenant is imperative in several ways:

1. Divine Promise: God's covenant with Abraham includes remarkable promises. He pledged that Abraham's descendants would be as numerous as the stars in the sky and that He would give them the land of Canaan. This divine commitment is pivotal in shaping the destiny of the Israelites.

2. Foundational Faith: Abraham's faith in God and his willingness to obey the divine call to leave his homeland and trust in the covenant are integral to the narrative. This faith serves as a model for believers and emphasizes the importance of unwavering trust in God's promises.

3. Sign of the Covenant: Circumcision is a physical sign of the covenant, symbolizing the commitment of Abraham's descendants to God's promises. It is a practice that has profound implications for identity and faith within the Abrahamic tradition.

The Terms of the Covenant:

The terms of the covenant between God and Abraham are outlined in several key passages in the Book of Genesis. One significant passage that describes the terms of the covenant is found in Genesis 15:

Genesis 15:5-7 (ESV):

"And he brought him outside and said, 'Look toward heaven, and number the stars if you are able to number them.' Then he said to him, 'So shall your offspring be.' And he believed the Lord, and he counted it to him as righteousness."

These verses illustrate the promise of numerous descendants as a central term of the covenant. Additionally, the covenant includes the promise of land, which is reiterated in later passages.

Circumcision, introduced in Genesis 17, serves as another key term of the covenant. Abraham and his male descendants are instructed to circumcise themselves as a physical sign of their commitment to the covenant.

The terms of the covenant involve promises of descendants and land, as well as the practice of circumcision as a sign of commitment. These terms are integral to the narrative and continue to be of great significance within the Abrahamic faith traditions.

Genesis 15:

The covenant between God and Abraham is introduced in Genesis 15. This pivotal event serves as a foundational moment in the relationship between God and Abraham.

Promise of Descendants:

In Genesis 15:5, God brought Abraham outside and directed his gaze toward the night sky. He said, "Look toward heaven, and number the stars, if you are able to number them." This celestial imagery was used to symbolize the promise of numerous descendants. God assured Abraham that his offspring would be as innumerable as the stars in the sky. This promise held profound significance for Abraham, who, at the time, was without an heir.

Promise of Land:

The covenant not only included the assurance of a multitude of descendants but also a pledge of land. In Genesis 15:18-21, God stated, "To your offspring, I give this land, from the river of Egypt to the great river, the river Euphrates." God specified the boundaries of the land that He would grant to Abraham's descendants, and this region would become known as the land of Canaan.

Abraham's Response:

Abraham's response to this covenant was one of faith and trust. Genesis 15:6 emphasizes his unwavering belief in God's promises: "And he believed the Lord, and he counted it to him as righteousness." Abraham's faith was counted as righteousness, highlighting the importance of trust in God's covenant within the Abrahamic tradition.

The Significance:

The covenant between God and Abraham marked a turning point in the patriarchal narrative. It reinforced the special relationship between God and Abraham, setting the stage for the fulfillment of the divine promises. This covenant was foundational to the identity and destiny of the Israelites and played a central role in shaping the course of history and faith within the Abrahamic traditions.

The terms of the covenant, including the promise of numerous descendants and the land of Canaan, carried profound implications for the future of Abraham's family and their relationship with God. This divine covenant is a testament to the enduring nature of God's promises and the pivotal role of faith within the biblical narrative.

Circumcision, as a sign of the covenant between God and Abraham's descendants, holds deep significance within the Abrahamic traditions. It serves as a physical and symbolic representation of their commitment to God and His promises. Here's how circumcision functions as a sign of the covenant:

1. Physical Mark of Commitment: Circumcision involves the removal of the foreskin from the male reproductive organ. This physical act is performed as a mark of commitment to God and the covenant. It signifies the

willingness to follow God's command and be set apart as part of the covenant community.

2. Identity and Inclusivity: Circumcision is a defining feature of identity within the Abrahamic faith traditions. It signifies one's belonging to the covenant people and is a rite of passage for male members of the community. It serves as a symbol of inclusion, marking those who have entered into the covenant.

3. Obedience to God's Command: The practice of circumcision reflects obedience to God's explicit command, as outlined in Genesis 17:10-14. Abraham and his descendants were instructed to circumcise themselves and their male offspring on the eighth day of life. This act of obedience reinforced their commitment to God and the terms of the covenant.

4. Continuity of the Covenant: Circumcision is a tradition passed down through generations. Each generation's adherence to this practice serves as a reminder of the enduring nature of the covenant and its promises. It connects present and future generations to the covenant established with Abraham.

5. Purification and Holiness: In some Abrahamic traditions, circumcision is associated with spiritual purification and holiness. It represents the removal of

impurities and a commitment to living a life in accordance with God's commandments.

6. Covenant of the Heart: While circumcision is a physical act, it also symbolizes the need for an inward transformation and commitment to God. In some Abrahamic traditions, it is emphasized that true circumcision should occur in the heart, signifying a person's inner dedication to God.

Circumcision, as a sign of the covenant, underscores the tangible and symbolic aspects of faith within the Abrahamic traditions. It represents commitment, identity, obedience, and continuity, all while serving as a potent reminder of the enduring relationship between God and the covenant people.

The profound significance of the covenant between God and Abraham is central to the narrative of faith, emphasizing themes of unwavering commitment and the enduring nature of God's promises. The practice of circumcision, as a sign of the covenant, serves as a pivotal element in the identity and faith of Abraham's descendants. This chapter explores the deep meaning of the covenant and the lasting impact of circumcision within the patriarchal narrative.

Faith and Commitment:

Abraham's unwavering faith and trust in God played a crucial role in the establishment of the covenant. His willingness to obey the divine call and embrace the covenant exemplifies the importance of faith within the Abrahamic traditions. The covenant is built on the bedrock of trust, reflecting the faith that God's promises will be fulfilled.

Enduring Promises:

God's covenant with Abraham is marked by enduring promises. The assurance of numerous descendants and the land of Canaan symbolizes God's commitment to fulfilling His word. These promises, which extend through generations, underscore the enduring nature of God's faithfulness.

Circumcision as Identity and Commitment:

Circumcision is a physical and symbolic embodiment of the covenant. It marks the commitment of Abraham's descendants to God and His promises. This act of obedience is a defining feature of identity within the Abrahamic traditions, signifying belonging to the covenant community.

Obedience to Divine Command:

Circumcision, as an act of obedience to God's explicit command, underscores the importance of following divine guidance. It serves as a tangible expression of faith and submission to God's will.

Continuity and Remembrance:

Circumcision's continuity through generations ensures that the covenant and its significance are never forgotten. Each generation's adherence to this practice is a powerful reminder of the enduring relationship between God and the covenant people.

The covenant between God and Abraham is a testament to the profound themes of faith, commitment, and the unwavering nature of God's promises. It highlights the transformative power of trust and the enduring legacy of faith within the Abrahamic traditions. The practice of circumcision, as a sign of the covenant, remains an integral aspect of identity and faith, serving as a constant reminder of the enduring commitment between God and Abraham's descendants within the patriarchal narrative.

CHAPTER 06

SACRIFICE OF ABRAHAM – WAS IT ISAAC OR ISHMAEL?

This Chapter is crucial for both Muslims and Christians. This Chapter serves as a decimating factor. It decimates the lies for the truth to triumph. It makes a decision based on evidence to reveal wherein lies the truth. Is it in Islam or Christianity?

Two opposing systems of values cannot be equally true. One or the other has to be. This Chapter is not written as an intellectual exercise in some mind games to amuse ourselves nor is it written to criticize the other for the joy of criticizing. No, it is written for the sole purpose of earnestly securing our salvation – our eternal salvation. If you are Muslim, please read this article objectively with an unbiased mind. This could be one of the most important decisions that you ever made in your life. This could be your first step in the right direction in the pursuit of salvation – your salvation. If you believe you have unshakable faith in Islam, then we dare you to read this article right through to the end. We dare you based on love.

Jews, Christians, and Muslims agree that Abraham was a righteous man with outstanding faith. This is seen in Abraham's willingness to sacrifice his only begotten son. All three religions do not dispute this fact. While Jews and Christians are unified on the identity of the sacrificial child, Islam disagrees. The Holy Bible identifies the sacrificial child as Isaac.

Genesis 22:1-2: Now after these things, it came about that the true God put Abraham to the test. Accordingly, he said to him: "Abraham!" And Abraham replied: "Here I am!" And God went on to say: "Take, please, your son, your only son whom you so love, Isaac, and make a trip to the land of Moriah and there offer him up as a burnt offering on one of the mountains that I shall designate to you."

Muslims say that the sacrificial son was Ishmael. The idea that Ishmael was the sacrificial son is based mainly on the Muslim misunderstanding of the phrase *"only son"* in the Genesis account. They assert that since Abraham was asked to offer his only son, it has to be Ishmael since he was the only son of Abraham for fourteen years. As such, they claim that it would be impossible for Isaac to be addressed as the only son of Abraham. Is their claim true?

But before we get to the bottom of this misunderstanding of Muslims and touch on the issue of the identity of the sacrificial son, it must be emphasized that no matter who the son was that Abraham offered as a sacrifice, Muslims are in error. They are in error if it was Isaac. And they are still in error if it was Ishmael. Muslims will do well if they do not raise this issue in the first place. It is a lose-lose situation for Muslims. Why do we say that? Carefully consider the shaky position of the Muslims when they challenge the authority of the Holy Bible regarding the identity of the sacrificial son.

The Muslim Dilemma:

The sacrificial account of Abraham's son is found in the Book of Genesis. Genesis is the first of the five Books of Moses which are collectively known as the Torah. Let us now see what the Qur'an testifies about the Torah:

Surah 5:44: "Lo! We did reveal the Torah, wherein is guidance and a light." (Pickthall)

Surah 5:68: Say (O Muhammad SAW) "O people of the Scripture (Jews and Christians)! You have nothing as regards guidance till you act according to the Taurat (Torah), the Injeel (Gospel)." (Hilali-Khan)

The Qur'an testifies that the Torah was revealed by Allah. According to the Qur'an, the Torah is the inspired "Word of Allah." And the Qur'an also commands Jews and Christians to abide by the teachings of the Torah and the Gospel. It tells them: "You have nothing as regards guidance till you act according to the Torah and the Gospel."

Well, what do Christians find when they obey this commandment of Allah to follow the teachings of the Torah and the Gospel?

The Torah distinctively identifies Isaac as the sacrificial son offered by Abraham. The sacrificial choice of God is identified as Isaac.

To counter this clear identity of Isaac as the sacrificial son in the Torah, Muslims came up with the blasphemous allegation that the Torah and the Gospel in our present Bible are not the originals but are corruptions of the originals. Without any evidence whatsoever to substantiate their claim, they say that some Jewish scribes changed the original reading from Ishmael to Isaac in the Torah. The change was supposedly carried out to glorify their Jewish heritage through Isaac. Well, let us see what Allah has to say on this matter. The Qur'an testifies:

Surah 10:64: "None can change the Words of Allah. This is indeed the Supreme Triumph." (Pickthall)

"No change can there be in the words of Allah. This is indeed the supreme felicity." (Yusuf Ali)

The Qur'an itself testifies: *"None can change the Words of Allah."* And since the Qur'an acknowledges that the Torah and the Gospel are the *"Words of Allah,"* it would require a denial of the Qur'an itself to believe that they have been changed through corruption. If the claim of corruption by Muslims is true, then Allah must be a lying impostor for making false claims to the contrary in the Qur'an.

The Qur'an becomes a lie for teaching that the Words of Allah cannot be changed.

If Muslims truly believe that the Qur'an is the Word of Allah, then they must accept as true that according to the Qur'an, no one can change the Torah or the Gospel. This means the sacrificial son has to be Isaac as the Torah testifies. On the other hand, if Muslims choose to believe that the Torah has been changed through corruption and the sacrificial son was Ishmael, then Muslims must also accept as true that Allah is a lying impostor and the Qur'an is a lie. Muslims do not have the luxury of believing that the Bible has become corrupted without first conceding that Allah lied in the Qur'an.

The only possibility for the sacrificial son to be Ishmael is for the *"Words of Allah"* to be changed in the Torah. Muslims cannot have it both ways. They cannot maintain their sacred belief that the *"Words of Allah"* will remain unchanged for all eternity and at the same instance believe that the Jews changed the Torah. Muslims are taught to believe that Ishmael was the sacrificial son. Therefore, they are in error if the sacrificial son was Isaac. And it has to be Isaac if the Qur'an is to be believed when it says: *"None can change the Words of Allah."* Muslims are still in error if it was Ishmael because it shows that they are worshipping a false deity who deceitfully told them that *"None can change the Words of Allah"* when in reality, the Jews changed the Torah. They changed the name of Ishmael to Isaac in the Torah.

It will be impossible for Muslims to believe that Ishmael was a sacrificial son without denying the teachings of Allah in the Qur'an. It would be impossible for Muslims to believe it was Ishmael without accepting it as true that the Jews changed the name from Ishmael to Isaac in the Book of Allah. Therefore, the only option left for Muslims to hold on to their cherished assumption that it was Ishmael is to accept that the Jews changed the unchangeable Scriptures of Allah.

Thus, no matter who the son was, Muslims are in error. For Muslims to believe that it was Ishmael is the greater error because it means that they must now accept as true that Allah is a lying impostor. Period.

Muslims should stop spreading lies about the Holy Bible. It will be beneficial for them to seriously consider the stern warning that Allah gives to all those who spread such lies about the integrity of the Holy Bible:

Surah 40:70-72: Those who gave the lie to this Book and all the Books which We had sent with Our Messengers shall soon come to know the Truth when fetters and chains shall be on their necks, and they shall be dragged into boiling water, and cast into the Fire. (Maududi)

Muslims should heed this warning. If Muslims are serious about Allah, then they must also take his warning seriously.

Of course, we do not believe that the Torah or the Gospel was inspired by Allah as the Qur'an claims. The true inspiration behind the Torah and the Gospel is none other than Jehovah – the God of Abraham, Isaac, and Jacob. Our reason for using the Qur'an to substantiate our argument is not because we believe in it but because Muslims believe in it. We used the Qur'an to prove to Muslims that their own sacred book not only confirms the integrity of the Holy Bible but it also proves their claim that the sacrificial son was Ishmael, is erroneous.

We are assured by Jehovah, blessed be his name, that to time indefinite the Holy Bible will be kept pure and it will be kept above the reach of those who intend to corrupt it:

Psalm 119:89: "Forever, O Jehovah, Your Word is firmly fixed in the heavens."

It is commonly believed in the Muslim world today that when God commanded Abraham to sacrifice his son, that son was Ishmael – the son of his slave-woman Hagar. However, finding not a single shred of evidence in the Qur'an to sustain their claim, Muslims try to deceptively use the account in the Bible to support their argument. For example, since the Bible states that God commanded Abraham to offer his *"only son"* as a sacrifice, Muslims argue that this could not be Isaac as he was never an only child seeing that Ishmael was born fourteen years before him.

However, the very verse in the Bible, which Muslims try so desperately to use to support their claim, clearly identifies Isaac by name as the sacrificial son. But Muslims deliberately exclude this vital piece of information in their argument.

Well, are Muslims correct in their belief that it was Ishmael who was the one offered by Abraham to be sacrificed? We like to take on a challenge with Muslims. Since the Bible identifies Isaac as the sacrificial son, can Muslims do the same by using the Qur'an only to prove that it was Ishmael? They cannot.

The arguments presented in this article are built progressively. Therefore, it is vital to read through to the end of this article to know for a certainty without a doubt who this sacrificial son of Abraham was. Was it Isaac or Ishmael?

First, let us read what the Bible says about this event:

Genesis 22:1-2: Now after these things, it came about that the true God put Abraham to the test. Accordingly, he said to him: "Abraham!" And Abraham replied: "Here I am!" And God went on to say: "Take, please, your son, your only son whom you so love, Isaac, and make a trip to the land of Moriah and there offer him up as a burnt offering on one of the mountains that I shall designate to you."

Genesis 22:9-13: Finally they reached the place that the true God had designated to him, and Abraham built an altar there and set the wood in order and bound Isaac his son hand and foot and put him upon the altar on top of the wood. Then Abraham put out his hand and took the slaughtering knife to kill his son. But Jehovah's angel began calling to him out of the heavens and saying: "Abraham, Abraham!" And Abraham answered: "Here I am!" And God went on to say: "Do not put out your hand against the boy and do not do anything at all to him, for now, I do know that you are God-fearing in that you have not withheld your son, your only one, from me." At that Abraham raised his eyes and looked and there, deep in the foreground, there was a ram caught by its horns in a thicket. So Abraham went and took the ram and offered it up for a burnt offering in place of his son.

For the full account of this event, please read Genesis 22:1-18. The above Biblical account of the sacrificial offering of Abraham's son appears in just one passage in the entire Qur'an. It begins with Abraham speaking:

Surah 37:100-113: "O my Lord! Grant me a righteous (son)!" So we gave him the <u>good news of a boy</u> ready to suffer and forbear. Then, when (the son) reached (the age of serious) work with him, he said: "O my son! I see in vision that I offer thee in sacrifice: now see what is thy view!" (The son) said: "O my father! Do as thou art commanded: thou wilt find me, if God so wills one practicing Patience and Constancy!"

So when they had both submitted their wills (to God), and he had laid him prostrate on his forehead (for sacrifice), We called out to him, "O Abraham! Thou hast already fulfilled the vision!" — thus indeed do We reward those who do right. For this was a trial — and We ransomed him with a momentous sacrifice: and We left (this blessing) for him among generations (to come) in later times: "Peace and salutation to Abraham!"

Thus indeed do We reward those who do right. For he was one of Our believing Servants. And We gave him the good news of Isaac — a prophet, — one of the Righteous. We blessed him and Isaac: but of their progeny are (some) that do right, and (some) that obviously do wrong, to their own souls. (Yusuf Ali)

Before we analyze the above Qur'anic verses in detail, it is important to note that when we compare the Biblical account with the one in the Qur'an, we find the following omissions in the Qur'an. While the Bible identifies the sacrificial son as Isaac, the Qur'an does not mention the name of the son. And while the Bible mentions the mountainous region of Moriah as the site of the sacrifice, the Qur'an does not give the slightest hint as to where this sacrifice was to take place.

The above Qur'anic verses tell us that Allah *"ransomed him (Abraham's son) with a momentous sacrifice."* Although Islam completely rejects the Biblical doctrine of substitutionary atonement, namely the ransom sacrifice of Jesus Christ, we observe that the doctrine of the ransom as a release from death is strongly supported in the above account in the Qur'an. The fact that the Qur'an testifies that Allah redeemed Abraham's son using a substitutive sacrifice, should awaken Muslims to seriously consider the doctrine of the ransom sacrifice of Jesus Christ.

As to why a *"momentous sacrifice"* has to be paid as a ransom by Allah for the release of Abraham's son and how this prefigures the Ransom Sacrifice of Jesus Christ.

Let us now analyze the above Qur'anic verses carefully. Note that at the very beginning of this Qur'anic account, the *"good news"* or promise of a boy was given to

Abraham. (Surah 37:101) The account then continues by saying that when this promised child reached the age of serious work, he accompanied his father Abraham to be offered as a sacrifice. The account concludes with Allah saying: *"And We gave him the good news of Isaac – a prophet, – one of the Righteous. We blessed him and Isaac."*

The account in the Qur'an makes it very clear that the child who was promised *"good news"* to Abraham was the very child who later accompanied him to be offered as a sacrifice. And towards the end of the account, the Qur'an specifically names Isaac as the promised child. While Isaac's name is mentioned twice in this only account of the sacrifice in the Qur'an, there is no mention of Ishmael at all. This is indeed amazing considering how overzealous some Muslims have been in their attempts to prove that the sacrificial son was Ishmael and not Isaac. Isaac is the only one named in the Qur'an as the child specifically promised to Abraham – a fact which the Qur'an agrees with the Bible.

Given the fundamental truth that the Qur'an does not say which son was taken up to be sacrificed, is it not presumptuous for Muslims to fault the Bible's clear statement that the son who was offered to be sacrificed was Isaac? Muslim readers of the Qur'an can only search in vain for the name of Ishmael in the entire account of Surah 37:100-113 where the story of the sacrifice is told. Therefore, no Muslim can honestly make a dogmatic statement that it was Ishmael in the light of the Qur'an's complete silence on the actual identity of the son. In contrast, the Bible identifies the son by name:

Genesis 22:2: And He went on to say: "Take, please, your son, your only son whom you so love, Isaac, and make a trip to the land of Moriah and there offer him up as a burnt offering on one of the mountains that I shall designate to you.

The hypocrisy of the Muslim claim can be seen by the fact that while they hang on desperately to the Bible's statement that God commanded Abraham to offer his *"only son,"* they deliberately choose to ignore the fact that the very same verse they quote to support their claim, clearly identifies the son by name as *"Isaac."* Should not it be either all or nothing? And Allah agrees. He gives the following warning to those who resort to this subtle form of deception:

Surah 2:85: "Then is it only a part of the Book that you believe in, and do you reject the rest? But what is the reward for those among you who behave like this but disgrace in this life? – And on the Day of Judgment they shall be consigned to the most grievous penalty. For Allah is not unmindful of what you do." (Yusuf Ali)

This Qur'anic verse was revealed as a warning for all those who commit the grave error of accepting only parts of the inspired Scriptures while rejecting others. And as proven earlier, the Qur'an testifies to the fact that the Torah is the inspired Word of God. Besides the account in the Hebrew Scriptures (Old Testament), the Christian Greek Scriptures (New Testament) also positively identify the sacrificial son of Abraham as Isaac:

Hebrews 11:17-18: "By faith Abraham, when he was tested, as good as offered up Isaac. He who had received the promises was ready to offer up his only begotten son of whom it was said, "Through Isaac shall your descendants be named."

James 2:21: Was not Abraham our father declared righteous by works after he had offered up Isaac his son upon the altar?

In all the passages of the Bible, it is quite plainly stated that Abraham offered up Isaac on the altar. Yet in the only passage in the Qur'an where the sacrifice is discussed, there is not a single mention of Ishmael. The Qur'an does not identify who the son was. Therefore, while there is a double testimony in the Bible that the son was Isaac, both from the Hebrew and the Christian Greek Scriptures, there is no such testimony in the Qur'an that it was Ishmael.

This lack of a clear identity in the Qur'an led to wide disagreement among early Muslim commentators as to who the son was. Although for expediency the Muslim world today unanimously acknowledges Ishmael as the sacrificial son, there was much dispute in the early days of Islam on the subject with many renowned scholars of the Qur'an accepting that it was Isaac. A Muslim writer candidly admits:

Haykal, "The Life of Muhammad," p. 25:

The Qur'an did not mention the name of the sacrificial son, and hence Muslim historians disagree in this regard.

While acknowledging the conflicting views in Islam regarding this very issue, Al-Tabari who is considered as one of the premiere Islamic historians, gave his scholarly view on this matter.

Al-Tabari, "The History of al-Tabari," Volume II, Prophets and Patriarchs, p. 32:

"The earliest sages of our Prophet's nation disagree about which of Abraham's two sons it was that he was commanded to sacrifice. Some say it was Isaac, while others say it was Ishmael. Both views are supported by statements related to the authority of the Messenger of God.

If both groups of statements were equally sound, then — since they both came from the Prophet — only the Qur'an could serve as proof that the account naming Isaac is the more truthful of the two."

This means that if Muslims were to undertake an impartial and honest study of the Qur'an, they would have to agree that it was Isaac who was the chosen sacrifice. As an aside, please note how the above historical account reveals that Muhammad gave conflicting views. The above account says that *"both groups of statements…came from the Prophet."* As a result, Muslims became divided in their opinion as to who the son was. And Muslims are willing to stake their lives by following a man who is unsure about the revelations of God.

Well, what was Al-Tabari's reason to conclude that the evidence pointed to Isaac as the sacrificial son? Let us hear from the great Scholar himself.

Al-Tabari, The History of al-Tabari, Volume II, Prophets and Patriarchs, p. 89:

"As for the above-mentioned proof from the Qur'an that it really was Isaac, it is God's word that informs us about the prayer of His friend Abraham when he left his people to migrate to Syria with Sarah. Abraham prayed, 'I am going to my Lord who will guide me. My Lord! Grant me a righteous child.' This was before he knew Hagar, who was to be the mother of Ishmael. After mentioning this prayer, God goes on to describe the prayer and mentions that he foretold Abraham that he would have a gentle son. God also mentions Abraham's vision of himself sacrificing that son when he was old enough to walk with him.

The Book does not mention any tidings of a male child given to Abraham except in the instance where it refers to Isaac, in which God said, 'And his wife, standing by laughed when we gave her tidings of Isaac, and after Isaac, Jacob,' and 'Then he became fearful of them.' They said. 'Fear not!' and gave him tidings of a wise son. Then his wife approached, moaning, and smote her face, and cried, 'A barren old woman.' Thus, wherever the Qur'an mentions God giving tidings of the birth of a son to Abraham, it refers to Sarah (and thus to Isaac) and the same must be true of God's words 'So we gave him tidings of a gentle son', as it is true of all such references in the Qur'an."

Al-Tabari had valid reasons to conclude that the son was Isaac. He based his conclusions on the fact that the Qur'an *"does not mention any tidings of a male child given to Abraham except in the instance where it refers to Isaac."* And since the account in Surah 37:101-102 clearly states that it was the promised child who accompanied Abraham to be sacrificed, then it must surely be Isaac.

Al-Tabari also stated the following:

"That ram remained in custody with God until He let it go as Isaac's ransom." (The History of Al-Tabari: General Introduction and From the Creation to the Flood, Volume 1, p. 310)

Let us look into an incident during the early days of Islam. This incident clarifies who it was that the early Companions of Muhammad believed to be the sacrificial son of Abraham.

Mishkat Al-Masabih, Book 14, Chapter 4, Section 3:

"Muhammad b. al-Muntashir told of a man who vowed to sacrifice himself if God rescued him from his enemy. He consulted Ibn 'Abbas who told him to consult Masruq, and when he consulted him he replied, 'Do not sacrifice yourself, for if you are a believer you will kill a believing soul, and if you are an infidel you will hasten to hell; but buy a ram and sacrifice it for the poor, for Isaac was better than you and he was ransomed with a ram." He told Ibn 'Abbas and he replied, 'This is the decision I wanted to give

you." Razin transmitted it. (Mishkat Al-Masabih English Translation With Explanatory Notes by Dr. James Robson, Volume I, p. 733)

Ibn Abbas was a paternal cousin of Muhammad and a great scholar of Islam. So we are not dealing here with some stage-entertaining Muslim apologists but with the testimonies of the great Muslim scholars. Scholars who not only lived during the time of Muhammad but who were also his close Companions.

Gibb and Kramers, A Shorter Encyclopaedia of Islam, p. 175:

As the Qur'an verse does not state which son was to have been sacrificed, many Muslim theologians refer to the intended sacrifice to Ismail. …But it may be said that the oldest tradition — al-Tha`labi expressly emphasises the ashab and tabi`un, i.e. the Companions of the Prophet and their successors from `Umar b. al-Khattab to Ka`b al-Ahbar — did not differ from the Bible on this question.

As stated above, the earlier Companions of Muhammad, including the rightly guided Caliphs such as Caliph Umar, believed that it was Isaac who was the intended sacrifice. While Islam is divided, no such disagreement has ever existed between the Jews and Christians. It is universally believed without dissent by Jews and Christians that it was Isaac. It is only in Islamic history that one finds confusion regarding the identity of the son.

Now ponder deeply on the following reasoning. If the son to be sacrificed is truly Ishmael, then the omission of the name of the son in the Qur'an is truly a strange anomaly given one very important factor. It is inconsistent with the qualities of an all-knowing God. Why do we say that? Muslims claim that the name of Ishmael was deliberately removed from the Bible and replaced with Isaac. If Allah is the author of the Qur'an, surely he must have known that it is emphatically taught in both the Old and the New Testament that it was Isaac who was offered as a sacrifice. As a result, this "erroneous teaching" came to be universally accepted. Since the Qur'an was revealed centuries after the completion of the Bible, surely an all-knowing Allah would have corrected the error with an equally emphatic statement in the Qur'an that it was Ishmael. Why was Ishmael's name not mentioned at all in the sacrificial account in the Qur'an? Why did Allah remain silent?

In other words, since there is a double testimony from both the Old and the New Testament that the son was Isaac, and if the Qur'an had come to clarify any previous errors as Muslims claim, it surely would have named Ishmael if he was indeed the chosen victim. In the light of the prevailing belief that it was Isaac, the omission in the Qur'an regarding the identity of the son is inexcusable if it was Ishmael.

Since Ishmael is named directly in the Qur'an in other instances such as he being Allah's helper in the building of the Ka'ba, is it not strange that Allah omitted his name when it matters most? Is it not strange that Allah missed out on the best opportunity to correct an obvious error in the Bible?

Is not the omission of Ishmael's name in the entire Surah (the 37th Surah in the Qur'an) all the more significant, especially when this Surah covers a number of the stories of the earlier prophets who are all specifically mentioned by name?

Surah 37 mentions many of the earlier prophets by name.

Names such as Noah (Surah 37:75, 79), Abraham (Surah 37:83, 104, 109), Isaac (Surah 37:112, 113), Moses (Surah 37:114, 120), Aaron (Surah 37:114, 120), Elijah (Surah 37:123, 130), Lot (Surah 37:133) and Jonah (Surah 37:139).

Therefore, the omission of the name of Ishmael in the only passage in the Qur'an where the event of the sacrifice is recorded is astonishing. It is truly astonishing if Ishmael was indeed the chosen son. In fact, in the entire Surah, you cannot find the name of Ishmael. The fact of the matter is that Surah 37 has nothing to do with Ishmael. Surah 37:100-113 is just a repeat of the account regarding Abraham and Isaac in Genesis 22.

Muslims try to come up with all kinds of excuses to prove that the sacrificial son was Ishmael. Failing to find any, they even try to divide what is otherwise a clear segment in the Qur'an on a single subject of the sacrificial offer of Abraham. For example, some Muslims argue that since *"the good news of Isaac"* is announced only after the account of the sacrifice, therefore the preceding account of the sacrifice must refer to another son of Abraham, namely Ishmael. In other words, Muslims are saying that while the two verses (Surah 37:112-113) which appear after the account refer to Isaac, the preceding twelve verses (Surah 37:100-111) are speaking about Ishmael.

Their argument is seriously flawed for numerous reasons. Firstly, Surah 37:100-111 does not mention the name of Ishmael at all. Additionally, the very mention of Isaac by name, immediately following the sacrifice will only serve to distort one's understanding of the narrative that precedes it if it did involve another son. It is hard to believe that the sacrifice refers to Ishmael when Isaac is promptly mentioned twice by name in the very verses that follow the proposed sacrifice. But there is more.

There is an unmistakable link between the phrasing of the sentences that precede the command to sacrifice and the phrasing of the sentences that follow immediately after the command to sacrifice. Take note of the remarkable similarities in the wordings regarding the promised child that precede the passage of the command to sacrifice with the wordings regarding the promised child immediately after the passage of the command to sacrifice. Let us analyze the Qur'anic passage to expose the fallacy of the Muslim argument.

Firstly, we noticed that immediately before the subject of the sacrifice was introduced, a son was promised to Abraham: *"So We gave him the good news of a boy ready to suffer and forbear." (Surah 37:101).*

Immediately after the narration of the sacrifice, Isaac is mentioned by name as the promised child to Abraham: "We gave him the good news of Isaac." (Surah 37:112).

Can you notice the symmetry between the two phrases? Now when we connect the two phrases it reads as: *"So We gave him the good news of a boy ready to suffer and forbear. We gave him the good news of Isaac."*

Therefore, the claim by Muslims that the stated *"good news of a boy"* at the beginning of the sacrificial account refers to Ishmael is deceptive. This is all the more true as the name of Ishmael appears nowhere, whereas *"the good news of Isaac"* is mentioned clearly by name in this account. Furthermore, *"the good news of Isaac"* is mentioned in three other accounts in the Qur'an while none whatsoever about Ishmael. The three other accounts can be found in Surah 11:70-71 which refers to Isaac as the promised child by name and, Surah 15:53 and Surah 51:28-29 which refer to Isaac as the promised child by clear unmistakable references. Therefore, we have four accounts in the Qur'an that speak about Isaac as the promised child and none at all about Ishmael in the entire Qur'an.

Secondly, there is also a clear symmetry between the phrase before the sacrificial account, *"So when they had both submitted their wills." (Surah 37:103)*, and the phrase after the sacrificial account, *"We blessed him and Isaac." (Surah 37:113)*.

Once again when we connect the two phrases it reads as: *"So when they had both submitted their wills. We blessed him and Isaac."*

Thus, it can be seen that the Qur'an is actually speaking of only one single incident and that only one single individual (Isaac) apart from Abraham is involved in the entire account of Surah 37:100-113. It is also significant to note that there is no word in the text, such as *"then" (Arabic: thumma)*, to denote a separation between the narration of the sacrifice and the narration of Isaac.

It can be seen that the Muslim argument that Ishmael must have been the sacrificial son because the story of the sacrifice precedes the mention of Isaac is highly erroneous upon closer analysis. It should be noted that the idea that the sacrifice incident is divided into two sections is concocted by Muslims and is not based on facts. Certainly, the complete omission of Ishmael's name in the passage considerably undermines the dogmatic Muslim claim that he was the sacrificial son.

We will now discuss the issue as to why Isaac is addressed as the "only son" of Abraham in the Genesis account.

Why Isaac is recognized as the "Only Son" of Abraham:

Since Muslims claim that the phrase *"only son"* can only apply to Ishmael, it is important to explain how this phrase applies exclusively to Isaac and not to Ishmael. It is equally important to explain how Isaac can rightfully be considered the only son of Abraham for various legitimate reasons. Both the Holy Bible and the Qur'an affirm the unique status of Isaac. Isaac was addressed as the only son of Abraham for the following reasons:

The Only promised child of Abraham:

Both the Holy Bible and the Qur'an testify that Isaac was the only promised child of Abraham:

Genesis 17:15-21: And God went on to say to Abraham: "As for Sarai your wife, you must not call her name Sarai, because Sarah is her name. And I will bless her and also give you a son from her, and I will bless her and she shall become nations; kings of peoples will come from her." At this, Abraham fell upon his face and began to laugh and to say in his heart: "Will a man a hundred years old have a child born, and will Sarah, yes, will a woman ninety years old give birth?"

After that Abraham said to the true God: "O that Ishmael might live before you!" To this God said: "Sarah your wife is indeed bearing you a son, and you must call his name Isaac. And I will establish my covenant with him for a covenant to time indefinite to his seed after him. But as regards Ishmael I have heard you. Look! I will bless him and will make him fruitful and will multiply him very, very much. He will certainly produce twelve chieftains, and I will make him become a great nation. However, my covenant I shall establish with Isaac, whom Sarah will bear to you at this appointed time next year."

And Isaac was also the only name of a promised child of Abraham that is expressly stated in the Qur'an:

Surah 11:69-71: There came Our messengers to Abraham with glad tidings. They said, "Peace!" He answered, "Peace!" …And his wife was standing (there), and she laughed: But We gave her glad tidings of Isaac, and after him, of Jacob. (Yusuf Ali)

Provided below is another Surah that speaks of the *"glad tidings of a son."* The angels who visited Abraham and Sarah gave them the good news of a promised son. Even though the following Qur'anic verses do not mention Isaac by name, we can be very certain that this account is in fact about him because the account is a repeat of the same incident as the above Surah where the promised child of Abraham is identified as Isaac:

Surah 51:24-30: Has the story reached thee, of the honored guests of Abraham? Behold, they entered his presence, and said: "Peace!" He said, "Peace!" …They said, "Fear not, and they gave him glad tidings of a son endowed with knowledge. But his wife came forward (laughing) aloud: she smote her forehead and said: "A barren old woman!" They said, "Even so has thy Lord spoken: and He is full of Wisdom and Knowledge." (Yusuf Ali)

The only *"barren old woman"* who was given *"glad tidings of a son"* was Sarah. And she is described here as the wife of Abraham. Therefore, the son mentioned here can only be Isaac and no other. The Bible teaches that Isaac was the only promised child of Abraham and as we can see, the Qur'an agrees with this fact. The important point for Muslims to reflect on is the fact that the Qur'an repeatedly mentions Isaac as the only promised child of Abraham. And as evidenced earlier, great Muslim scholars such as al-Tabari agree on this fact.

The only Son who was conceived miraculously:

Furthermore, it was not Ishmael but Isaac who was conceived with the aid of God's miraculous power:

Genesis 17:15-17: And God went on to say to Abraham: "As for Sarai your wife, you must not call her name Sarai, because Sarah is her name. And I will bless her and also give you a son from her, and I will bless her and she shall become nations; kings of peoples will come from her." At this, Abraham fell upon his face and began to laugh and to say in his heart: "Will a man a hundred years old have a child born, and will Sarah, yes, will a woman ninety years old give birth?"

Genesis 18:11-14: And Abraham and Sarah were old, being advanced in years. Sarah had stopped having menstruation. Hence Sarah began to laugh inside herself, saying: "After I am worn out, shall I have pleasure, my lord being old besides?" Then Jehovah said to Abraham: "Why was it that Sarah laughed, saying, 'Shall I really and truly give birth although I have become old?' Is anything too extraordinary for Jehovah? At the appointed time I shall return to you, next year at this time, and Sarah will have a son."

In agreement with the Bible, the Qur'an also recognizes this fact regarding God's intervention to revitalize the dead womb of Sarah. The Qur'an states the following:

Surah 11:72-73: She said, 'Alas for me! How am I to bear a child when I am an old woman, and my husband here is an old man? That would be a strange thing!' They said, 'Are you astonished at what

The above verses from both the Bible and the Qur'an tell us that Sarah no longer could have children. A miracle will have to be performed for her to have children. Jehovah God will have to bring her womb to life again for her to conceive a child. And Jehovah did this by giving Sarah and Abraham the ability to conceive Isaac through his divine intervention. In contrast, Ishmael was born normally without any divine intervention.

The only legitimate Son of Abraham:

Isaac was the only legitimate son of Abraham when God commanded him to make the sacrificial offering. Isaac was begotten through Sarah, the legitimate wife of Abraham. Thus, Isaac was a legitimate son of Abraham. Furthermore, the Bible reveals that Hagar, the mother of Ishmael, was a *"maidservant"* of the wife of Abraham. It was only because Sarah herself could not bear children that she said to Abraham:

Genesis 16:2-3: 'Please have relations with my servant. Perhaps I can have children using her." So Abram listened to what Sarai said. ....Abram's wife Sarai took her Egyptian servant Hagar and gave her to her husband Abram as a wife.

The expression here is intended to mean that she gave Hagar to her husband to cohabit with him and not to make her a second wife as Muslims often claim these verses imply. This fact is seen in how Hagar is addressed by Abraham even after she bore him a son. When Hagar conceived Ishmael and looked in contempt upon Sarah, Abraham responded to Sarah by saying:

Genesis 16:6: "Look! Your maidservant is at your disposal. Do to her what is good in your eyes."

And when Hagar was in the wilderness, an angel of the true God appeared to her. Notice how he addressed Hagar when he spoke to her years after she bore Abraham a son:

Genesis 16:8: "Hagar, the maidservant of Sarai, just where have you come from and where are you going?"
And later this angel admonished her:

Genesis 16:9: "Return to your mistress and humble yourself under her hand."

Notice carefully, that this angel of the true God never once addressed Hagar as the wife of Abraham. He did not say return to your husband but return to your mistress. Ibn Sa'd's Kitab al-Tabaqát al-Kabir is one of the earliest works on the biographical literature of Islam and a valuable source of information for the students of Islamic history as well as scholars engaged in Islamic research. This Islamic source confirms that Hagar was only a servant in Abraham's household whom Sarah gave to him solely to bear him a son:

Ibn Sa'd, Kitab al-Tabaqat al-Kabir, Vol. 1, p. 41:

Then he called Hajar who was the most trustworthy of his servants and he bestowed her (Hajar) on her (Sarah) and gave her clothes; subsequently, Sarah made a gift of her (Hajar) to Ibrahim who cohabited with her and she bore Ismail who was the eldest of his children.

Quite clearly Hagar was never regarded as the wife of Abraham but only as the maidservant of Sarah. This would make Ishmael an illegitimate son of Abraham. Thus, it was quite proper for God to speak of Isaac as Abraham's only son, namely his only legitimate son through his legitimate wife Sarah.

For Muslims who claim that Hagar was the legitimate wife of Abraham, we challenge them to produce a single verse from the Qur'an to back their claim. As shown above, Hagar was no more than a maidservant of Sarah. She was given to Abraham by Sarah herself for the single purpose of bearing a child for Abraham and Sarah. However, what makes the Muslim claim a preposterous lie is the complete absence of any mention of Hagar in the Qur'an – even of the slightest reference to her. It is truly astonishing how Muslims can come up with this claim. The entire Qur'an has no reference to Hagar whatsoever, let alone by name. Is not the complete silence about Hagar in the Qur'an, a clear testimony that the Qur'an recognizes Sarah alone as the wife of Abraham?

Surah 11:71: "And his wife was standing there, and she laughed: But we gave her glad tidings of Isaac, and after him, of Jacob."

As the son is specifically named here as Isaac, there can be little doubt as to the identity of his mother. Why did not the Qur'an say, *"And one of his wives was standing there"*? If Hagar had also been one of Abraham's wives, would it not be more appropriate to say, *"And one of his wives was standing there."* Or would it not be more proper to identify her as *"his wife Sarah."* However, when the Qur'an purely speaks of Abraham's wife in the singular, without any form of identification, it recognizes the fact that Abraham had only one wife and that wife was Sarah.

A very important fact to bear in mind is that when the promise of Isaac was made to Abraham and Sarah, Ishmael had already been born. Therefore, for Surah 11:71 to refer to Sarah at this point as Abraham's only wife is a clear testimony that Hagar was not one of his wives. It must be remembered that there is no mention whatsoever neither by name nor by reference of Hagar in the Qur'an. This is indeed a strange omission if she was also a wife of Abraham. If a Muslim were to read through the entire Qur'an without reference to any external source, he would not be able to guess that there was another woman in Abraham's life.

The only woman mentioned in the above Qur'anic account is described as the single wife of Abraham and she is expressly described as the mother of Isaac. If Sarah is mentioned alone as the wife of Abraham in the Qur'an and also described as such in the Bible, can there be any objection to the description of Isaac as *your only son* in Genesis 22:2? Since Sarah is the only legitimate wife of Abraham, is it not perfect to describe their son Isaac as Abraham's only son?

Additionally, since Sarah alone is mentioned in the Qur'an as the single wife of Abraham, would God announce to Abraham the birth of a righteous boy conceived through an illegitimate union with a slave woman? (Surah 37:101) This is especially true as no mention whatsoever of this woman appears in the Qur'an. The only son promised to Abraham in the Qur'an is Isaac and Surah 37:102 makes it quite plain that it was this very same promised son who was commanded to be sacrificed.

Therefore, the only conclusion we can draw is that the sacrificial son has to be Isaac and no other. It is only the popular sentiment of the Muslims that it was Ishmael and that is for obvious reasons. We have seen just how the promise of a son to Abraham was inextricably linked to the subsequent command to sacrifice him. Where do think these evidences point to? Do they point to Isaac or Ishmael? The answer is obvious.

The only Son who lived with Abraham:

Isaac was the only son who lived with Abraham. Many years before the event when Abraham offered Isaac as a sacrifice on Mount Moriah, Ishmael and his mother Hagar had already been sent away. Ishmael was no longer a member of Abraham's household. Thus, Abraham was left with Isaac as his only son.

Genesis 21:14: So Abraham got up early in the morning and took bread and a skin water bottle and gave it to Hagar, setting it upon her shoulder, and the child, and then dismissed her. And she went her way and wandered about in the wilderness of Beersheba.

Since the Qur'an completely omits any mention of Hagar, Muslims are in no position to dispute the above-stated Biblical statement.

The Quran recognizes Isaac as the Only Son:

Many verses in the Qur'an prove that it recognizes Isaac as the unique son of Abraham. Surah 29:27 is one such verse. It is one of the most significant verses in the Qur'an. It is significant because it shows the descendants of which son of Abraham God selected to establish the Prophethood and the Scriptures.

Surah 29:27: And We bestowed upon Abraham (a son) Isaac, and (a grandson) Jacob, and caused Prophethood and Revelation to continue among his progeny. And We gave him his reward in this world, and verily, in the life to come, he shall be among those who have perfected their personality. (Shabbir Ahmed)

"And We bestowed on (Abraham) Isaac and Jacob, and We established the Prophethood and the Scripture among his seed, and We gave him his

reward in the world, and lo! In the Hereafter he verily is among the righteous." (Pickthall)

Why was the name of Ishmael completely left out in this Qur'anic verse? This is very significant because Ishmael was the older son – the firstborn. Notice the order of the genealogy in this Qur'anic verse – Abraham (Father), Isaac (Son) and Jacob (Grandson).

Does not this Qur'anic verse identify and recognize Isaac as the only son of Abraham? Why? Is it not because he is the only legitimate son of Abraham? Is it not because he is the only promised son who is worthy of the *Prophethood and the Scripture* to be established through his genealogy?

This Qur'anic verse states emphatically that the *"Prophethood"* and the *"Scripture"* will be established to only those who came from the lineage of Abraham through Isaac. Thus, the Qur'an itself confirms the superiority of Isaac over Ishmael. Is it not strange that Ishmael is completely disregarded in this blessed privilege of God? Why was he not recognized as the son of Abraham when it matters most? Does not this prove that it is therefore legitimate for Isaac to be addressed as the *"only son"* in the Holy Bible?

The message in Surah 29:27 is certainly an emphatic statement. This Qur'anic verse is very important because it establishes the identity of the sacrificial son with utmost certainty. To understand the importance of Surah 29:27, we must first consider the Covenant that God made with Abraham immediately after he proved faithful to the sacrificial test:

Genesis 22:15-18: And Jehovah's angel called to Abraham a second time from the heavens, saying: "By myself I swear,' declares Jehovah, 'that because you have done this and you have not withheld your son, your only one, I will surely bless you and I will surely multiply your seed like the stars of the heavens and like the grains of sand on the seashore, and your seed will take possession of the gate of his enemies. And using your seed, all nations of the earth will obtain a blessing for themselves because you have listened to my voice.'"

Because of Abraham's obedience, God promised to bless his offspring. And Surah 29:27 confirms that in keeping with his promise, God blessed the nation who came through the lineage of Isaac. It emphatically states: *"And We bestowed on Abraham, Isaac, and Jacob, and We established the Prophethood and the Scripture among his <u>seed</u>, and We gave him his reward in the world."*

Centuries before the arrival of the Qur'an, the Holy Bible confirms this vital truth that God in keeping true to his Covenant with Abraham established it through the Nation of Israel – the descendants of Isaac:

Romans 9:4-5: Who, as such, are Israelites, to whom belong the adoption as sons and the glory and the covenants and the giving of the Law and the sacred service and the promises; to whom the forefathers belong and from whom the Christ sprang according to the flesh: God, who is over all, be blessed forever. Amen.

And the Qur'an agrees once again with this profound truth:

Surah 45:16: And verily We gave the Children of Israel the Scripture and the Command and the Prophethood, and provided them with good things and favored them above all peoples." (Pickthall)

Hence, it must be concluded that the intended sacrificial victim could only have been Isaac and not Ishmael. The Qur'an confirms the superiority of Isaac over Ishmael. It may surprise Muslims to learn that in many instances where Abraham is mentioned along with his son and especially so when it is stated in a genealogical manner, the name of Ishmael is completely ignored in the Qur'an. In these instances, Isaac is recognized as the only son of Abraham in the Qur'an. So not only the Bible but the Qur'an also recognizes Isaac as the only son of Abraham in many of its verses. We will now provide a few examples of such verses in the Qur'an:

Surah 6:84: We gave (Abraham) Isaac and Jacob. Both had received Our guidance. Noah received Our guidance before Abraham and so did his descendants: David, Solomon, Job, Joseph, Moses, and Aaron. This is the reward for the righteous people. (Muhammad Sarwar)

Surah 19:49-50: When (Abraham) rejected his people and what they worshipped instead of God, We gave him Isaac and Jacob and made both of them Prophets. We granted them Our blessing and high renown. (Muhammad Sarwar)

Was not Ishmael the firstborn son of Abraham? Was he not given as a son to Abraham? Why then do the above Qur'anic verses totally discount Ishmael as one of the sons given to Abraham? Is it not ironic that these Qur'an verses completely ignore the older son of Abraham and instead mention the younger son as the immediate son of Abraham? What is the Qur'an's reason for doing so?

Surah 38:45-47: (Muhammad), recall Our servants Abraham, Isaac, and Jacob, all of whom possessed virtuous hands and clear visions. We gave them this pure distinction because of

Again, we notice that the Qur'an does not take Ishmael into account as one of the sons of Abraham. The younger son is mentioned once again as the immediate son of Abraham and even the name of the grandson is included but not the name of the firstborn son. Why? There are other verses such as these in the Qur'an but the above is sufficient to prove our point.

Thus, considering all the evidence, we can see that the Muslim claim that Ishmael was the sacrificial son has no solid evidence to substantiate it. The plain statements in the Bible that it was Isaac must refer to the Qur'an's vague and confusing treatment of the identity of the son whom Abraham was commanded to sacrifice.

The Qur'an's teaching to a large extent underlines the superiority of Isaac over Ishmael. His lineage was God's choice for the fulfillment of his eternal promises. This leads us to the conclusion that it was Isaac who was commanded to be sacrificed as a sign of the coming sacrifice of Abraham's greater son, Jesus Christ. The offering of Isaac served as a sign of the greater sacrifice in the person of Christ Jesus. A sacrifice that was to serve as God's way of opening the doors of his salvation to the world of mankind. As Isaac was preferred over Ishmael, likewise Jesus Christ must be preferred over Muhammad. Jesus Christ is the true son of Abraham – the true Sacrifice of God whom Isaac prefigured.

Matthew 1:1: "The book of the history of Jesus Christ, son of David, son of Abraham."

As stated earlier, Islamic sources themselves testify that owing to the lack of a clear identity in the Qur'an, there were disagreements among early Muslims as to who the sacrificial son was. If you, as a Muslim, still have doubts regarding the identity of the sacrificial son, then we encourage you to consider the advice given in your sacred text:

Surah 10:94: So if you are in doubt, (O Muhammad), about that which We have revealed to you, then ask those who have been reading the Scripture before you. (U. Muhammad, Sahih International)

Muhammad was commanded by Allah to consult the people *"who have been reading the Scripture"* that was revealed *"before"* him when he had doubts. Those who had been reading the Scriptures before the time of Muhammad were the Christians. They read the Holy Bible. Yes, even your Prophet was directed by Allah to seek spiritual assistance from the Christians as a means of clearing his doubts. You should do the same. And Christians will be glad to assist you. They will gladly enlighten you that it was Isaac – without a doubt.

CHAPTER 07

THE SACRIFICIAL CHOICE: ISAAC OR ISHMAEL?

Jews, Christians, and Muslims agree that Abraham was a righteous man with outstanding faith. This is seen in Abraham's willingness to sacrifice his only begotten son. All three religions do not dispute this fact. While Jews and Christians are unified on the identity of the sacrificial child, Islam disagrees. The Bible identifies the sacrificial child as Isaac. However, Muslims say that it was Ishmael.

But even before we develop our arguments on the issue of the identity of the sacrificial son, it must be emphasized that no matter who the son was that Abraham offered to be sacrificed, Muslims are still in error. They are in error if it was Isaac. And they are still in error if it was Ishmael. Muslims will do well if they do not raise this issue in the first place. It is a lose-lose situation for Muslims. Why do we say that? Carefully consider how the shaky position of the Muslims when they challenge the authority of the Bible regarding the identity of the Son.

The Muslim Dilemma:

The sacrificial account of Abraham's son is found in the Book of Genesis. Genesis is one of the five Books of Moses which are collectively known as the Torah. Let us now see what the Qur'an says about the Torah:

Surah 5:44: "Lo! We did reveal the Torah, wherein is guidance and a light." (Pickthall)

Surah 5:68: Say (O Muhammad SAW) "O people of the Scripture (Jews and Christians)! You have nothing as regards guidance till you act according to the Taurat (Torah), the Injeel (Gospel)." (Hilali-Khan)

The Qur'an testifies that the Torah was revealed by Allah. Therefore, according to the Qur'an, the Torah is the inspired "Word of Allah." And the Qur'an also commands Jews and Christians to abide by the teachings of the Torah and the Gospel. It tells them: "You have nothing as regards guidance till you act according to the Torah and the Gospel."

Well, when Jews and Christians obey this commandment of Allah to follow the teachings of the Torah and the Gospel, what do they find? Both the Torah and the Gospel specifically identify Isaac as the son who was offered by Abraham as a sacrifice. The sacrificial choice was identified as Isaac.

To counter this clear identity of Isaac as the sacrificial son in the Bible, Muslims came up with the outrageous allegation that the Torah and the Gospel in our present Bible are not the originals but are corruptions of the originals. They claim that to glorify their ancestor ship through Isaac, the Jews changed the name from Ishmael to Isaac in the Torah. Well, let us see what Allah has to say on this matter. The Qur'an testifies:

Surah 10:64: "No change can there be in the words of Allah. This is indeed the supreme felicity." (Yusuf Ali)
"None can change the Words of Allah. This is indeed the Supreme Triumph." (Pickthall)

The Qur'an itself says: *"None can change the Words of Allah."* And since the Qur'an teaches that the Torah and the Gospel are the *"Words of Allah,"* it would require a denial of the Qur'an itself to believe that they have been changed through corruption. If the claim of corruption by Muslims is true, then Allah is a lying impostor for making false claims to the contrary in the Qur'an. The Qur'an becomes a lie for teaching that the Words of Allah cannot be changed.

If Muslims believe that the Qur'an is the true Word of Allah, then they must also believe that according to the Qur'an, it is impossible to corrupt the Torah and the Gospel. This means the sacrificial son has to be Isaac as testified in both the Torah and the Gospel. However, if the Torah and the Gospel have been changed through corruption and the sacrificial son was Ishmael, then Muslims must accept the fact that Allah is a liar and the Qur'an is a lie. To say that the Bible has been permitted by Allah to become corrupted is to believe that Allah lied in the Qur'an.

The Muslim position that Ishmael is the sacrificial son is possible only if the *"Words of Allah"* have been changed in the Torah. Muslims cannot have it both ways. They cannot believe that the *"Words of Allah"* cannot be changed and at the same instance believe that the Jews changed the Torah. Muslims are in error if it was Isaac because they strongly believe that Ishmael was the sacrificial son. And Muslims are still in error if it was Ishmael because it shows that they are worshipping a false deity. A deity who lyingly told them that *"None can change the Words of Allah"* when the Jews changed the Torah.

It will be impossible for Muslims to believe that Ishmael was the sacrificial son without denying the teachings of Allah in the Qur'an. It would be impossible for Muslims to believe it was Ishmael without accepting it as true that the Jews changed the name from Ishmael to Isaac in the Book of Allah. Therefore, the only option left for Muslims to hold on to their cherished assumption that it was Ishmael is to accept that the Jews changed the unchangeable Scriptures of Allah. Thus, no matter who the son was, Muslims are in error. For Muslims to believe that it was Ishmael is the greater error because it means Allah is a lying impostor. Period.

Muslims should stop spreading lies about the Holy Bible. It will be beneficial for them to seriously consider the stern warning that Allah gives to all those who spread such lies about the integrity of the Holy Bible:

Surah 40:70-72: Those who gave the lie to this Book and all the Books which We had sent with Our Messengers shall soon come to know the Truth when fetters and chains shall be on their necks, and they shall be dragged into boiling water, and cast into the Fire. (Maududi)

Of course, we do not believe that the Torah or the Gospel was inspired by Allah as the Qur'an claims. The true inspiration behind the Torah and the Gospel is none other than Jehovah – the God of Abraham, Isaac, and Jacob.

Therefore, our reason for using the Qur'an is not because we believe in it but because Muslims believe in it. It was a necessary approach that had to be used to prove to Muslims that their own sacred book confirms the integrity of the Holy Bible. Ironically, the Qur'an itself proves the Muslim argument to be erroneous.

We are assured by Jehovah, blessed be his name, that to time indefinite the Holy Bible will be kept pure and it will be kept above the reach of those who intend to tarnish it: *Psalm 119:89: "Forever, O Jehovah, Your Word is firmly fixed in the heavens."*

There is no further need to discuss this issue. However, we will do so for the benefit of our readers, especially our Muslim readers. It is commonly believed in the Muslim world today that when God commanded Abraham to sacrifice his son, that son was Ishmael – the son of his slave-woman Hagar. However, finding not a single shred of evidence in the Qur'an to sustain their claim, Muslims try to make deceptive use of the account in the Bible to support their argument. For example, since the Bible states that God commanded Abraham to offer his only son as a sacrifice, Muslims argue that this could not be Isaac as he was never an only child seeing that Ishmael was born fourteen years before him. However, they deliberately exclude the fact that the very same account identifies who the son was.

Well, are Muslims correct in their belief that it was Ishmael who was the one offered by Abraham to be sacrificed? We like to take on a challenge with Muslims. Since the Bible identifies Isaac as the sacrificial son, can Muslims use the Qur'an only to prove that it was Ishmael?

The arguments presented in this article are built progressively. Therefore, it is vital to read through to the end of this article to know for certainty who this sacrificial son of Abraham was. Was it Isaac or Ishmael?

First, let us read what the Bible says about this event:

Genesis 22:1-14: Now after these things, it came about that the true God put Abraham to the test. Accordingly, he said to him: "Abraham!" And Abraham replied: "Here I am!" And God went on to say: "Take, please, your son, your only son whom you so love, Isaac, and make a trip to the land of Moriah and there offer him up as a burnt offering on one of the mountains that I shall designate to you."

So, Abraham got up early in the morning and saddled his ass and took two of his attendants with him and Isaac his son, and he split the wood for the burnt offering. Then he rose and went on the trip to the place that the true God designated to him. It was first on the third day that Abraham raised his eyes and began to see the place from a distance. Abraham now said to his attendants: "You stay here with the ass, but I and the boy want to go on over there and worship and return to you."

After that Abraham took the wood of the burnt offering and put it upon Isaac his son and took in his hands the fire and the slaughtering knife, and both of them went on together. And Isaac began to say to Abraham his father: "My father!" In turn, he said: "Here I am, my son!" So he continued: "Here are the fire and the wood, but where is the sheep for the burnt offering?" To this, Abraham said: "God will provide himself the sheep for the burnt offering, my son." And both of them walked on together.

Finally, they reached the place that the true God had designated to him, and Abraham built an altar there and set the wood in order and bound Isaac his son's hand and foot, and put him upon the altar on top of the wood. Then Abraham put out his hand and took the slaughtering knife to kill his son. But God began calling to him out of the heavens and saying: "Abraham, Abraham!" And Abraham answered: "Here I am!" And God went on to say: "Do not put out your hand against the boy and do not do anything at all to him, for now I do know that you are God-fearing in that you have not withheld your son, your only one, from me."

At that Abraham raised his eyes and looked and there, deep in the foreground, there was a ram caught by its horns in a thicket. So Abraham went and took the ram and offered it up for a burnt offering in place of his son. And Abraham began to call the name of that place Jehovah-Jireh. This is why it is customarily said today: "In the mountain of Jehovah it will be provided."

The above Biblical account of the offering of Abraham's son as a sacrifice appears in just one passage in the entire Qur'an. Here is what the Qur'an says about the event. We will quote it in full.

Surah 37:100-113

It begins with Abraham speaking:

Surah 37:100-113: "O my Lord! Grant me a righteous (son)!" So we gave him the <u>good news of a boy</u> ready to suffer and forbear. Then, when (the son) reached (the age of serious) work with him, he said: "O my son! I see in vision that I offer thee in sacrifice: now see what is thy view!" (The son) said: "O my father! Do as thou art commanded: thou wilt find me, if God so wills one practicing Patience and Constancy!" So when they had both submitted their wills (to God), and he had laid him prostrate on his forehead (for sacrifice), We called out to him, "O Abraham! Thou hast already fulfilled the vision!" — thus indeed do We reward those who do right. For this was a trial — and We ransomed him *with a momentous sacrifice: and We left (this blessing) for him among generations (to come) in later times: "Peace and salutation to Abraham!"*

Thus indeed do We reward those who do right. For he was one of Our believing Servants. And We gave him the good news of Isaac – a prophet, – one of the Righteous. We blessed him and Isaac: but of their progeny are (some) that do right, and (some) that do wrong, to their souls. (Yusuf Ali)

Before we analyze the above Qur'anic verses in detail, it is important to note that when we compare the Biblical account with the one in the Qur'an, we find the following omissions in the Qur'an. While the Bible identifies the sacrificial son as Isaac, the Qur'an does not mention the name of the son. And while the Bible mentions the mountainous region of Moriah as the site of the sacrifice, the Qur'an does not give the slightest hint as to where this sacrifice was to take place.

The above Qur'anic verse tells us that Allah *"ransomed him (Abraham's son) with a momentous sacrifice."* Although Islam completely rejects the Biblical doctrine of substitutionary atonement, namely the ransom sacrifice of Jesus Christ, the doctrine of the ransom as a release from death is strongly supported in the above account in the Qur'an. The fact that the Qur'an testifies that Allah redeemed Abraham's son using a substitutive sacrifice, should awaken Muslims to consider the doctrine of the ransom sacrifice of Jesus carefully. As to why a *"momentous sacrifice"* has to be paid as a ransom for the release of Abraham's son and how does this prefigure the Ransom Sacrifice of Jesus Christ?

Let us now analyze the above Qur'anic verses carefully. Note that at the very beginning of this account, the *"good news"* or promise of a boy was given to Abraham. (Surah 37:101) The account then continues by saying that when this promised child reached the age of serious work, he accompanied his father Abraham to be offered as a sacrifice. The account concludes with Allah saying: *"And We gave him the good news of Isaac – a prophet, – one of the Righteous. We blessed him and Isaac."*

The account in the Qur'an makes it very clear that the child who was promised *"good news"* to Abraham is the very child who accompanied him to be offered as a sacrifice. And towards the end of the account, the Qur'an specifically names Isaac as the promised child. While Isaac's name is mentioned twice in this only account of the sacrifice in the Qur'an, there is no mention of Ishmael at all. Thus, Isaac was the only one named in the Qur'an as the child specifically promised to Abraham – a fact which the Qur'an agrees with the Bible. What can we then understand from this account in the Qur'an? Where does the evidence point to? Do they point to Isaac or Ishmael? The answer is obvious.

The above Qur'anic verses are straightforward to understand but not so for Muslims. There are also other verses in the Qur'an which expressly state that the promised son was Isaac.

Surah 11:69-71: There came Our messengers to Abraham with glad tidings. They said, "Peace!" He answered, "Peace!" …And his wife was standing (there), and she laughed: But We gave her glad tidings of Isaac, and after him, of Jacob. (Yusuf Ali)

Though the following Qur'anic verses does not mention Isaac by name, we can be certain that this account is in fact about him because the verses are a repeat of the same incident as the above Surah where Isaac is identified by name:

Surah 51:24-30: Has the story reached thee, of the honored guests of Abraham? Behold, they entered his presence, and said: "Peace!" He said, "Peace!" …They said, "Fear not, and they gave him glad tidings of a son endowed with knowledge. But his wife came forward (laughing) aloud: she smote her forehead and said: "A barren old woman!" They said, "Even so has thy Lord spoken: and He is full of Wisdom and Knowledge." (Yusuf Ali)

The only *"barren old woman"* who was given *"glad tidings of a son"* was Sarah. And she is described here as the wife of Abraham. Therefore, the son mentioned here cannot be anyone other than Isaac. The important point for us to reflect on is the fact that the Qur'an repeatedly mentions Isaac as the promised child. The Bible teaches that Isaac was the only promised child of Abraham and as we can see, the Qur'an agrees with this fact.

Furthermore, it was not Ishmael but Isaac who was conceived with the aid of God's miraculous power:

Genesis 17:15-17: And God went on to say to Abraham: "As for Sar'ai your wife, you must not call her name Sar'ai, because Sarah is her name. And I will bless her and also give you a son from her, and I will bless her and she shall become nations; kings of peoples will come from her." At this, Abraham fell upon his face and began to laugh and to say in his heart: "Will a man a hundred years old have a child born, and will Sarah, yes, will a woman ninety years old give birth?"
Genesis 18:11-14: And Abraham and Sarah were old, being advanced in years. Sarah had stopped having menstruation. Hence Sarah began to laugh inside herself, saying: "After I am worn out, shall I have pleasure, my lord being old besides?" Then Jehovah said to Abraham: "Why was

it that Sarah laughed, saying, 'Shall I really and truly give birth although I have become old?' Is anything too extraordinary for Jehovah? At the appointed time I shall return to you, next year at this time, and Sarah will have a son."

In agreement with the Bible, the Qur'an also recognizes this fact regarding God's intervention to revitalize Sarah and Abraham. The Qur'an states the following:

Surah 11:72-73: She said, 'Alas for me! How am I to bear a child when I am an old woman, and my husband here is an old man? That would be a strange thing!' They said, 'Are you astonished at what God ordains? The grace of God and His blessings be upon you, people of this house! For He is worthy of all praise and glory.' (Abdel Haleem)

The above verses from both the Bible and the Qur'an tell us that Sarah no longer could have children. A miracle will have to be performed for her to have children. Jehovah God will have to bring her womb to life again for her to have a child. He is the One that gave Sarah and Abraham the ability to have Isaac. In contrast, Ishmael was born normally without any divine intervention.

The Bible states plainly that Isaac who was begotten through Sarah, the legitimate wife of Abraham, was the promised child. The Qur'an agrees with this testimony in the Bible. And since the Qur'anic narrative shows that it was the promised child who accompanied Abraham to be sacrificed, then it is evident that the Qur'an recognizes Isaac as the son who was offered to be sacrificed.

The Bible reveals that Hagar (Hajira in Islam), the mother of Ishmael, was a *"maidservant"* of the wife of Abraham. It was only because Sarah herself could not bear children that she said to Abraham:

Genesis 16:2-3: Please, have relations with my maidservant. Perhaps I may get children from her. Then Sarai took Hagar, her Egyptian maidservant, and gave her to Abram her husband as a wife.

The expression here is intended to mean that she gave Hagar to her husband to cohabit with him and not to make her a second wife to him as Muslims often claim these verses imply. This fact is seen in how Hagar is addressed by Abraham even after she bore him a son. When Hagar conceived and looked in contempt upon Sarah, Abraham responded:

Genesis 16:6: "Look! Your maidservant is at your disposal. Do to her what is good in your eyes."

And when Hagar was in the wilderness, an angel of the true God appeared to her. Notice how he addressed Hagar:

Genesis 16:8: "Hagar, the maidservant of Sarai, just where have you come from and where are you going?"
And later this angel admonished her:

Genesis 16:9: "Return to your mistress and humble yourself under her hand."

Notice carefully, that this angel of the true God never once addressed Hagar as the wife of Abraham. Ibn Sa'd's Kitab al-Tabaqát al-Kabir is one of the earliest works on the biographical literature of Islam and a valuable source of information for the students of Islamic history as well as scholars engaged in research. This Islamic source confirms that Hagar was only a servant in Abraham's household whom Sarah gave to him solely to bear him a son:

Ibn Sa'd, Kitab al-Tabaqat al-Kabir, Vol. 1, p. 41:
Then he called Hajar who was the most trustworthy of his servants and he bestowed her (Hajar) on her (Sarah) and gave her clothes;

subsequently, Sarah made a gift of her (Hajar) to Ibrahim who cohabited with her and she bore Ismail who was the eldest of his children.

Quite clearly Hagar was never regarded as the wife of Abraham but only as the maidservant of Sarah. Thus, it was quite proper for God to speak of Isaac as Abraham's only son, namely his only legitimate son through his wife Sarah.

Additionally, at the time when Abraham offered Isaac as a sacrifice on Mount Moriah, Ishmael and his mother Hagar had already been sent away many years before this event. Ishmael was no longer a member of Abraham's household. Thus, Abraham was left with Isaac as his only son.

Genesis 21:14: So Abraham got up early in the morning and took bread and a skin water bottle and gave it to Hagar, setting it upon her shoulder, and the child, and then dismissed her. And she went her way and wandered about in the wilderness of Beersheba.

It is futile for Muslims to even endeavor to fault the Bible's clear statement that the son who was offered to be sacrificed was Isaac. They should not even attempt to do so given the essential fact that the Qur'an does not say which son was to be sacrificed. Every Muslim reader of the Qur'an can only search in vain for the name of Ishmael in the account in Surah 37:100-113 where the story of the sacrifice is told. No Muslim can sincerely make a dogmatic statement that it was Ishmael in the light of the Qur'an's complete silence on the actual identity of the son.

The hypocrisy of the Muslim claim can be seen by the fact that while they desperately cling to the Bible's statement that God commanded Abraham to offer his only son, they deliberately choose to ignore the fact that the very same verse they quote to support their claim, clearly identifies the son by name as Isaac. It is either all or nothing.

Genesis 22:2: And He went on to say: "Take, please, your son, your only son whom you so love, Isaac, and make a trip to the land of Moriah and there offer him up as a burnt offering on one of the mountains that I shall designate to you.

Besides the account in Genesis (Old Testament), the Christian Greek Scriptures (New Testament) also positively identify the son whom God commanded Abraham to sacrifice as Isaac. The following two Biblical verses from the Christian Greek Scriptures prove this point:

Hebrews 11:17-18: By faith Abraham, when he was tested, offered up Isaac, and he who had received the promises was ready to offer up his only son, of whom it was said, "Through Isaac shall your descendants be named."

James 2:21: Was not Abraham our father justified by works when he offered his son Isaac upon the altar?

In all the passages of the Bible, it is quite plainly stated that Abraham offered up Isaac on the altar. Yet in the only passage in the Qur'an where the sacrifice is discussed, there is not a single mention of Ishmael. The Qur'an does not identify who the son was. Therefore, while there is a double testimony in the Bible, both from the Hebrew and the Christian Greek Scriptures that the son was Isaac, there is no such testimony in the Qur'an that it was Ishmael.

This lack of a clear identity in the Qur'an led to wide disagreement among Muslim commentators as to who the son was. Although for purposes of convenience today the Muslim world unanimously acknowledges Ishmael as the sacrificial son, there was much dispute in the early days of

Islam on the subject with many renowned Commentators of the Qur'an accepting that it was Isaac. A Muslim writer candidly admits:

Haykal, "The Life of Muhammad," p. 25:

The Qur'an did not mention the name of the sacrificial son, and hence Muslim historians disagree in this regard.

While acknowledging the conflicting views in Islam regarding this very issue, Al-Tabari, considered as one of the most prominent Islamic historians, gave his scholarly view on this matter.

Al-Tabari, The History of al-Tabari, Volume II, Prophets and Patriarchs p. 32:

"The earliest sages of our Prophet's nation disagree about which of Abraham's two sons it was that he was commanded to sacrifice. Some say it was Isaac, while others say it was Ishmael. Both views are supported by statements related to the authority of the Messenger of God. If both groups of statements were equally sound, then — since they both came from the Prophet — only the Qur'an could serve as proof that the account naming Isaac is the more truthful of the two."

This means that if Muslims were to undertake an impartial and honest study of the Qur'an, they would have to agree that Isaac was the chosen sacrifice. As an aside, notice how the above historical account reveals that Muhammad gave conflicting views. The above account says that *"both groups of statements…came from the Prophet."* As a result, Muslims became divided in their opinion as to who the son was. And Muslims are willing to stake their lives by following a man who is unsure about the revelations of God.

Well, what was Al-Tabari's reason to conclude that the evidence points to Isaac as the sacrificial son? Let us hear from the great Scholar himself.

Al-Tabari, The History of al-Tabari, Volume II, Prophets and Patriarchs, p. 89:

"As for the above-mentioned proof from the Qur'an that it was Isaac, it is God's word that informs us about the prayer of His friend Abraham when he left his people to migrate to Syria with Sarah. Abraham prayed, 'I am going to my Lord who will guide me. My Lord! Grant me a righteous child.' This was before he knew Hagar, who was to be the mother of Ishmael. After mentioning this prayer, God goes on to describe the prayer and mentions that he foretold Abraham that he would have a gentle son. God also mentions Abraham's vision of himself sacrificing that son when he was old enough to walk with him. The Book does not mention any tidings of a male child given to Abraham except in the instance where it refers to Isaac, in which God said, 'And his wife, standing by laughed when we gave her tidings of Isaac, and after Isaac, Jacob,' and 'Then he became fearful of them.' They said. 'Fear not!' and gave him tidings of a wise son. Then his wife approached, moaning, and smote her face, and cried, 'A barren old woman.' Thus, wherever the Qur'an mentions God giving tidings of the birth of a son to Abraham, it refers to Sarah (and thus to Isaac) and the same must be true of God's words 'So we gave him tidings of a gentle son', as it is true of all such references in the Qur'an."

Al-Tabari had valid reasons to conclude that the son was Isaac. He based his conclusions on the fact that the Qur'an *"does not mention any tidings of a male child given to Abraham except in the instance where it refers to Isaac."* And since the account in Surah 37:101-102 clearly states that it was the promised child who accompanied Abraham to be sacrificed, then it must surely be Isaac.

Al-Tabari also stated the following:

"…That ram remained in custody with God until He let it go as Isaac's ransom." (The History of Al-Tabari: General Introduction and From the Creation to the Flood, Volume 1, p. 310)

Let us look into an incident that clarifies as to who it was that the early Companions of Muhammad believed was the sacrificial son of Abraham.

Mishkat Al-Masabih, Book 14, Chapter 4, Section 3:

"Muhammad b. al-Muntashir told of a man who vowed to sacrifice himself if God rescued him from his enemy. He consulted Ibn 'Abbas who told him to consult Masruq, and when he consulted him he replied, "Do not sacrifice yourself, for if you are a believer you will kill a believing soul, and if you are an infidel you will hasten to hell; but buy a ram and sacrifice it for the poor, for Isaac was better than you and he was ransomed with a ram." He told Ibn 'Abbas and he replied, "This is the decision I wanted to give you." Razin transmitted it. (Mishkat Al-Masabih English Translation With Explanatory Notes by Dr. James Robson, Volume I, p. 733)

Ibn Abbas was a paternal cousin of Muhammad and a great scholar of Islam. So we are dealing here with the testimonies of the great Muslim scholars who not only lived during the time of Muhammad but who were also his close Companions.

Gibb and Kramers, A Shorter Encyclopaedia of Islam, p. 175:

As the Qur'an verse does not state which son was to have been sacrificed, many Muslim theologians refer the intended sacrifice to Ismail. …But it may be said that the oldest tradition — al-Tha`labi expressly* *emphasises the ashab and tabi`un, i.e. the Companions of the Prophet and their successors from `Umar b. al-Khattab to Ka`b al-Ahbar – did not differ from the Bible on this question.

As stated above, the earlier Companions of Muhammad, including the rightly guided Caliphs such as Caliph Umar, believed that it was Isaac who was the intended sacrifice. While Islam is divided, no such disagreement has ever existed between the Jews and Christians. It is universally believed without dissent that it was Isaac. It is only in Islamic history that one finds confusion regarding the identity of the son.

Now ponder deeply on the following important point. If the son to be sacrificed is truly Ishmael, then the omission of the name of the son in the Qur'an is truly strange given one very important factor. It is inconsistent with the qualities of an all-knowing God. Why do we say that? Muslims claim that the name of Ishmael was deliberately removed from the Bible and replaced with Isaac in the sacrificial account. If Allah is the author of the Qur'an, surely he must have known that it was emphatically taught in both the Old and the New Testament that it was Isaac who was offered to be sacrificed. And consequently, this came to be universally accepted. Since the Qur'an was revealed centuries after the completion of the Bible, surely an all-knowing Allah would have corrected the error with an equally emphatic statement in the Qur'an that it was Ishmael. Why did Allah remain silent?

In other words, since there is a double testimony from both the Old and the New Testament that the son was Isaac and if the Qur'an had come to clarify any previous errors as Muslims claim, it would surely have named Ishmael if he was the chosen victim. In the light of the prevailing belief that it was Isaac, the omission in the Qur'an regarding the identity of the son is inexcusable if it was indeed Ishmael.

Since Ishmael is named directly in the Qur'an in other instances such as being Allah's helper in the building of the Ka'ba, is it not strange that Allah omitted his name where it matters most? Is it not strange that Allah missed out on the best opportunity to correct an error in the Bible? Is not the omission of Ishmael's name in the entire Surah all the more significant, especially when this Surah covers a number of the stories of the earlier prophets who are all specifically mentioned by name?

Surah 37 mentions many of the earlier prophets by name. Names such as Noah (Surah 37:75, 79), Abraham (Surah 37:83, 104, 109), Isaac (Surah 37:112, 113), Moses (Surah 37:114, 120), Aaron (Surah 37:114, 120), Elijah (Surah 37:123, 130), Lot (Surah 37:133) and Jonah (Surah 37:139). Thus, the omission of the name of Ishmael in the only passage in the Qur'an where the event of the sacrifice is recorded is astonishing. It is truly astonishing if Ishmael was indeed the son who is to be offered. In fact, in the entire Surah, you cannot find the name of Ishmael. The fact of the matter is that Surah 37 has nothing to do with Ishmael. Surah 37:100-113 is just a repeat of the account regarding Abraham and Isaac in Genesis 22.

Muslims try to come up with all kinds of excuses to prove that the sacrificial son was Ishmael. They even try to divide what is otherwise a clear segment in the Qur'an on a single subject of the sacrificial offer of Abraham. For example, some Muslims argue that since *the good news of*

Isaac" is announced only after the account of the sacrifice, therefore the preceding account of the sacrifice must refer to another son of Abraham, namely Ishmael. In other words, Muslims are saying that while the two verses (Surah 37:112-113) which appears at the conclusion of the account refers to Isaac, the preceding twelve verses (Surah 37:100-111) is actually speaking about Ishmael.

Their argument is seriously flawed for numerous reasons. Firstly, Surah 37:100-111 does not mention the name of Ishmael at all. Additionally, the very mention of Isaac by name, immediately following the sacrifice will only serve to distort one's understanding of the narrative that precedes it if it did involve another son. It is hard to believe that the sacrifice refers to Ishmael when Isaac is promptly mentioned twice by name in the very verses that follow the proposed sacrifice. But there is more.

There is an unmistakable link between the phrasing of the sentences that precede the command to sacrifice and the phrasing of the sentences that follow immediately after the command to sacrifice. Take note of the remarkable similarities in the wordings regarding the promised child that precede the passage of the command to sacrifice with the wordings regarding the promised child immediately after the passage of the command to sacrifice. Let us analyze the Qur'anic passage to expose the fallacy of the Muslim argument.

Firstly, we noticed that immediately before the specific subject of the sacrifice was narrated, a son was promised to Abraham: *"So We gave him the good news of a boy ready to suffer and forbear." (Surah 37:101).*

Then immediately following the narration of the sacrifice, we read that Isaac was specifically promised to Abraham by name: *"We gave him the good news of Isaac." (Surah 37:112).*

Can you notice the symmetry between the above two phrases? Now when we connect the two phrases it reads as: *"So We gave him the good news of a boy ready to suffer and forbear. We gave him the good news of Isaac."*

It is important to note that nowhere in this Qur'anic passage is it ever stated that Ishmael was similarly promised to Abraham. His name is completely missing in the entire Surah. It is also vital not to forget that Isaac was specially mentioned by name as the promised child.

Secondly, there is also a clear symmetry between the earlier phrase, *"So when they had both submitted their wills." (Surah 37:103)* and the later phrase, *"We blessed him and Isaac." (Surah 37:113).*

Once again when we connect the two phrases it reads as: *"So when they had both submitted their wills. We blessed him and Isaac."*

As Abraham and Isaac *"had both submitted their wills"* to God – that one should sacrifice the other – God *"blessed him and Isaac."*

Thus, it can be seen that the Qur'an is speaking of only one single incident and that only one single individual (Isaac) apart from Abraham is involved in the account in Surah 37:100-113. It is also significant to note that there is no word in the text, such as *thumma (then),* between the story of the sacrifice and the mention of Isaac to separate the two subject matters under discussion.

The Muslim argument that Ishmael must have been the sacrificial son because the story of the sacrifice precedes the mention of Isaac is shown to be highly erroneous upon closer analysis. It should be noted that the idea that the sacrifice incident is divided into two sections is concocted by Muslims and is not based on facts. Certainly, the complete omission of Ishmael's name in the passage considerably undermines the dogmatic Muslim claim that he was the son who was commanded to be sacrificed.

Muslims also claim that Hagar was a legitimate wife of Abraham. As shown above, Hagar was no more than a maidservant of Sarah. She was given to Abraham by Sarah herself for the single purpose of bearing a child for Abraham and Sarah. Additionally, if the Muslim claim is true, the complete absence of any mention of Hagar in the Qur'an — even of the slightest reference to her is truly mind-boggling. The entire Qur'an has no reference to Hagar whatsoever, let alone by name. Is not the complete silence about Hagar in the Qur'an, a clear testimony that the Qur'an recognizes Sarah alone as the wife of Abraham? Let us analyze the Qur'anic verse which we quoted earlier:

Surah 11:71: "And his wife was standing there, and she laughed: But we gave her glad tidings of Isaac, and after him, of Jacob." As the son is specifically named here as Isaac, there can be little doubt as to the identity of his mother. Why did not the Qur'an say, *"And one of his wives was standing there"*? Now if Hagar had also been one of Abraham's wives, surely the text would have said, *"And one of his wives was standing there."* Either that or it would have at least identified her as *"his wife Sarah."* However, when the Qur'an purely speaks of

Abraham's wife in the singular, without any form of identification, it can be seen that it recognizes that Abraham had only one wife and that wife was Sarah.

When the promise of Isaac was made to Abraham and Sarah, Ishmael had already been born. Therefore, for Surah 11:71 to refer to Sarah at this point as Abraham's only wife is a clear testimony that Hagar was not one of his wives. It must be remembered that there is no mention of Hagar in the Qur'an whatsoever. This is indeed a strange omission if she also was a wife of Abraham. If a Muslim were to read through the Qur'an without reference to any external source, he would not be able to guess that there was another woman in Abraham's life.

The only woman mentioned in this Qur'anic account is described as the single wife of Abraham and she is expressly described as the mother of Isaac. If Sarah is mentioned alone as the wife of Abraham in the Qur'an and also described as such in the Bible, can there be any objection to the description of Isaac as *"your only son"* in Genesis 22:2? Since Sarah is the only legitimate wife of Abraham, is it not perfect to describe their son Isaac as Abraham's only son?

To recapitulate: In the Bible, the promise of God to Abraham is found in Genesis 17:19. And the Qur'an the promise was conveyed through the angelic messengers who came to destroy the people of Lot. (Surah 11:70-71) In both cases, it is the express promise of God that a son would be born to Abraham and that the son would be Isaac. In Surah 15:53 the narrative is repeated and the promise of a son is stated once again, though this time Isaac is not mentioned by name. The same goes for Surah 51:28-29 where once again the promise of a son to Abraham's only wife is repeated. Yusuf Ali, in a footnote, identifies it to be Sarah (*The Holy Qur'an*, p. 1424).

Finally, as we have seen, the promise of a son to Abraham appears again at the introduction of the story of the sacrifice (Surah 37:101), and a few verses later the promised son is specifically named Isaac. (Surah 37:112) There can be no doubt that Isaac is the only son promised to Abraham in the Qur'an and he must therefore be identified as the intended sacrificial son. It must be re-emphasized that nowhere in the Qur'an is Ishmael mentioned as the child of promise.

As Sarah alone is mentioned in the Qur'an as the single wife of Abraham, it is surely too hard to believe that God would announce to him the birth of a righteous boy (Surah 37:101), by an illegitimate union with a slave woman, especially as no mention whatsoever of this woman appears in the Qur'an. The only son promised to Abraham in the Qur'an is Isaac and Surah 37:102 makes it quite plain that it was this very same promised son who was commanded to be sacrificed. Therefore, the only conclusion we can draw is that the sacrificial son is Isaac. It is only the popular sentiment of the Muslims that it was Ishmael and that is for obvious reasons. We have seen just how the promise of a son to Abraham was inextricably linked to the subsequent command to sacrifice him.

Thus, considering all the evidence, we can see that the Muslim claim that Ishmael was the sacrificial son has no solid evidence to substantiate it. The plain statements in the Bible that it was Isaac must be preferred to the Qur'an's vague and confusing treatment of the identity of the son whom Abraham was commanded to sacrifice.

There is yet another text in the Qur'an that testifies to God's preference for Isaac over Ishmael. It is one of the most significant verses in the Qur'an. It is significant because it shows the descendants of which son of Abraham God selected to establish the Prophethood and the Scriptures.

Surah 29:27: And We bestowed upon Abraham (a son) Isaac, and (a grandson) Jacob, and caused Prophethood and Revelation to continue among his progeny. And We gave him his reward in this world, and verily, in the life to come, he shall be among those who have perfected their personality. (Shabbir Ahmed)

And We bestowed on (Abraham) Isaac and Jacob, and We established the Prophethood and the Scripture among his seed, and We gave him his reward in the world, and lo! In the Hereafter he verily is among the righteous. (Pickthall)

Why was Ishmael's name completely left out in this Qur'anic verse? This is very significant because Ishmael was the older son. Notice the order of the genealogy in this verse – Abraham, Isaac, and Jacob. Does not this Qur'anic verse identify and recognize Isaac as the only son of Abraham? Why? Is it not because he is the only legitimate son of Abraham? This Qur'anic verse also states emphatically that the *"Prophethood"* and the *"Scripture"* will be established to only those who came from the lineage of Abraham through Isaac. Thus, the Qur'an itself confirms the superiority of Isaac over Ishmael. Hence it must be concluded that as the intended sacrificial victim was announced to Abraham beforehand, it could only have been Isaac and not Ishmael. Centuries before the arrival of the Qur'an, the Holy Bible confirms this truth in Romans 9:4-5:

Who, as such, are Israelites, to whom belong the adoption as sons and the glory and the covenants and the giving of the Law and the sacred service and the promises; to whom the forefathers belong and from whom the Christ sprang according to the flesh: God, who is over all, be blessed forever. Amen.

And the Qur'an agrees:

Surah 45:16: And verily We gave the Children of Israel the Scripture and the Command and the Prophethood, and provided them with good things and favored them above all peoples." (Pickthall)

The Qur'an's teaching to a large extent underlines the superiority of Isaac over Ishmael and God's choice of his line for the fulfillment of his eternal promises. This leads us to the conclusion that it was Isaac who was commanded to be sacrificed as a sign of the coming sacrifice of Abraham's greater son, Jesus Christ, who would thereby open the doors of God's salvation to the world. As Isaac was preferred over Ishmael, likewise Jesus Christ must be preferred over Muhammad. Jesus Christ is the true son of Abraham – the true Sacrifice of God whom Isaac prefigured.

Matthew 1:1: "The book of the history of Jesus Christ, son of David, son of Abraham."

CHAPTER 08

THE DESTRUCTION OF SODOM AND GOMORRAH

The story of the destruction of Sodom and Gomorrah is a profound and impactful moment in the biblical narrative. This chapter explores the sinful cities of Sodom and Gomorrah and God's divine judgment upon them. It also delves into Abraham's plea for mercy, highlighting themes of justice, intercession, and divine judgment.

The Sinful Cities and God's Judgment:

The cities of Sodom and Gomorrah, as portrayed in the Bible, were notorious for their wickedness and sin. Their transgressions included inhospitality, violence, and sexual immorality. Their evil ways reached a point where divine intervention became necessary.

Genesis 18:20-21 (ESV):

"Then the Lord said, 'Because the outcry against Sodom and Gomorrah is great and their sin is very grave, I will go down to see whether they have done altogether according to the outcry that has come to me, and if not, I will know.'"

God's judgment was initiated in response to the outcry against the sinful cities. This divine intervention signifies God's commitment to justice and His willingness to hold the wicked accountable for their actions.

Abraham's Plea for Mercy:

In Genesis 18, as God's judgment on Sodom and Gomorrah was about to be executed, Abraham engaged in a poignant intercession. He implored God to spare the cities if righteous individuals were found within them. Abraham's plea for mercy highlights his compassion, his relationship with God, and his concern for the innocent amidst the judgment.

Genesis 18:32 (ESV):

"Then he said, 'Oh let not the Lord be angry, and I will speak again but this once. Suppose ten are found there.' He answered, 'For the sake of ten I will not destroy it.'"

Abraham's intercession raises questions about the nature of divine judgment, the role of righteous individuals in the face of evil, and the depths of God's mercy.

This chapter delves into the profound story of the destruction of Sodom and Gomorrah, emphasizing themes of justice, intercession, and divine judgment. It explores the consequences of sinful actions and the profound impact of Abraham's plea for mercy within the patriarchal narrative.

Introduction:

The story of the destruction of Sodom and Gomorrah is a significant and profound moment in the biblical narrative. It raises questions about divine justice, the consequences of sinful actions, and the power of intercession. To understand why these cities faced destruction and who lived there, we must delve into the historical and moral context of this account.

Why There Was a Destruction of Sodom and Gomorrah:

The destruction of Sodom and Gomorrah was initiated due to the overwhelming wickedness and sin that had permeated these cities. Their sins were grave, encompassing a range of transgressions, including inhospitality, violence, and sexual immorality.

Genesis 18:20 (ESV):

"Then the Lord said, 'Because the outcry against Sodom and Gomorrah is great and their sin is very grave, I will go down to see whether they have done altogether according to the outcry that has come to me, and if not, I will know.'"

God's decision to investigate the cities and execute judgment was based on the outcry of their grave sins. The people of Sodom and Gomorrah had reached a point of moral degradation that necessitated divine intervention.

Who Was Living There:

Sodom and Gomorrah were cities located in the region of the Jordan Valley, near the Dead Sea. They were inhabited by a population that had descended into sin and wickedness. The Bible does not provide detailed descriptions of the inhabitants but focuses on their collective moral decay.

The narrative primarily highlights Lot, Abraham's nephew, who had settled in Sodom. Lot and his family were among the inhabitants of these cities and would be affected by the impending judgment.

This chapter will further explore the nature of the sinful cities and the consequences of their actions, as well as the role of Abraham's intercession in the face of God's judgment. It delves into the themes of justice and divine intervention within the patriarchal narrative.

The sins of Sodom and Gomorrah, as depicted in the Bible, encompassed various transgressions, including inhospitality, violence, and sexual immorality. Here are some key references to these sins:

1. Inhospitality: In Genesis 19, two angels arrived in Sodom and were received by Lot, Abraham's nephew. Lot offered them hospitality by inviting them into his home. This event underscores the inhospitality and wickedness of the city's inhabitants, as the men of Sodom gathered outside Lot's house, demanding to have sexual relations with the visiting angels. This inhospitable and morally depraved behavior is a significant aspect of the city's sin.

Genesis 19:4-5 (ESV):

"But before they lay down, the men of the city, the men of Sodom, both young and old, all the people to the last man, surrounded the house. And they called to Lot, 'Where are the men who came to you tonight? Bring them out to us, that we may know them.'"

2. Violence: The people of Sodom were known for their violent tendencies. This is evident in their aggressive behavior toward Lot and the visiting angels. Their intent to harm and sexually assault the guests highlights the city's culture of violence.

Genesis 19:9 (ESV):

"But they said, 'Stand back!' And they said, 'This fellow came to sojourn, and he has become the judge! Now we will deal worse with you than with them.' Then they pressed hard against the man Lot, and drew near to break the door down."

3. Sexual Immorality: The sin of sexual immorality was another prominent aspect of the cities' wickedness. The people of Sodom pursued unnatural and immoral sexual acts, as evidenced by their demand to "know" the visiting angels in a sexual context.

Jude 1:7 (ESV):

"Just as Sodom and Gomorrah and the surrounding cities, which likewise indulged in sexual immorality and pursued unnatural desire, serve as an example by undergoing a punishment of eternal fire."

These sins had become so rampant and severe in Sodom and Gomorrah that they prompted divine judgment. The destruction of these cities, as described in the biblical narrative, serves as a testament to the consequences of moral degradation and the need for divine intervention in the face of such grave wickedness.

In Genesis 18:20-21, the Lord expresses His intention to investigate the situation in Sodom and Gomorrah. The reason given is the "outcry" against the cities, signifying the great wickedness and sin that had become prevalent there.

The Lord's decision to "go down to see" is a symbolic and anthropomorphic description, emphasizing His divine awareness of the sins committed in these cities and His commitment to justice.

The Lord meets Abraham first before the events involving the cities of Sodom and Gomorrah unfold. In the preceding verses of Genesis 18, the Lord, accompanied by two angels in the form of men, appears to Abraham near the oaks of Mamre. During this visit, the Lord shares His plan to investigate Sodom and Gomorrah due to their grave sin. Abraham then engages in intercession, pleading for the righteous within the cities. It is during this encounter that the Lord and Abraham engage in a dialogue, and Abraham's plea for mercy and intercession for the cities is initiated.

The initiation of God's judgment in response to the outcry against the sinful cities of Sodom and Gomorrah underscores several significant principles:

1. Divine Justice: The concept of divine justice is central in the Abrahamic faith traditions. God is portrayed as a just and righteous deity who upholds moral standards. When the outcry against the sins of Sodom and Gomorrah became great, it was seen as a breach of divine justice. God's response was to address and rectify this breach by holding the wicked accountable for their actions.

2. Moral Accountability: The notion of moral accountability is emphasized in the biblical narrative. The outcry against the cities signified that their sins had reached a level that required divine intervention. God's judgment reflects a commitment to ensuring that moral transgressions do not go unpunished. This is a fundamental aspect of God's character in the Abrahamic faith traditions.

3. Reinforcement of Moral Standards: God's response to the outcry serves as a reinforcement of moral standards within the biblical narrative. It underscores the importance of living in accordance with God's moral principles and the consequences of deviating from them. The judgment on Sodom and Gomorrah conveys the message that moral transgressions will not be tolerated.

4. Protection of the Innocent: God's judgment is not only a response to the sins of the cities but also a means of protecting the innocent. The narrative highlights the presence of righteous individuals within these cities, such as Lot. God's judgment serves to differentiate between the wicked and the righteous, illustrating His concern for the well-being of the innocent.

In summary, God's judgment initiated in response to the outcry against the sinful cities of Sodom and Gomorrah signifies His commitment to justice, moral accountability, and the enforcement of moral standards. It serves as a powerful reminder of the consequences of grave sin and the importance of upholding moral principles within the Abrahamic faith traditions.

Abraham's plea for mercy in the face of God's judgment on Sodom and Gomorrah reflects several significant aspects:

1. Compassion and Empathy: Abraham's plea is a testament to his compassion and empathy for the inhabitants of these cities, even in the face of their wickedness. He expressed concern for the potential presence of righteous individuals and demonstrated a desire for their salvation.

2. Relationship with God: Abraham's relationship with God played a pivotal role in his intercession. His dialogue with God in Genesis 18 reveals a level of intimacy and trust. Abraham approached God with a sense of familiarity and faith, which allowed him to make a direct appeal for mercy.

Genesis 18:23 (ESV):

"Then Abraham drew near and said, 'Will you indeed sweep away the righteous with the wicked?'"

3. Concern for the Innocent: Abraham's plea underscores his concern for the innocent individuals who might be living in the cities. He wanted to ensure that the righteous would not suffer the same fate as the wicked. This

reflects a sense of justice and a desire to protect those who were living righteously.

Genesis 18:25 (ESV):

"Far be it from you to do such a thing, to put the righteous to death with the wicked, so that the righteous fare as the wicked! Far be that from you! Shall not the Judge of all the earth do what is just?"

4. Faith in God's Character: Abraham's intercession is also rooted in his faith in God's character. He believed that God, as the "Judge of all the earth," would do what is just. His plea rested on the belief that God's justice would be carried out in a way that distinguished between the righteous and the wicked.

Abraham's plea for mercy is a poignant moment in the narrative, illustrating his deep compassion, his strong relationship with God, and his commitment to justice. It also serves as a model of intercession within the Abrahamic faith traditions, emphasizing the importance of prayer and advocacy on behalf of others, even in challenging circumstances.

Abraham's intercession in Genesis 18, particularly the dialogue highlighted in Genesis 18:32, raises profound questions about the nature of divine judgment, the role of righteous individuals in the face of evil, and the depths of God's mercy for several reasons:

1. The Nature of Divine Judgment:

Abraham's intercession challenges our understanding of divine judgment. It prompts us to contemplate whether God's judgment is absolute and unyielding or whether there is room for negotiation and intercession. By suggesting different hypothetical scenarios and the number of righteous individuals required to spare the cities, Abraham questions the nature of God's justice and whether it allows for mercy.

2. The Role of Righteous Individuals:

Abraham's intercession highlights the role of righteous individuals within a community facing judgment. It raises the question of whether the presence of even a few righteous people can influence the divine decision. It implies that the actions and righteousness of a minority may have the potential to impact the fate of the majority. This underscores the idea that the presence of righteousness can serve as a source of grace and protection for a community.

3. God's Mercy and Compassion:

The dialogue showcases the depths of God's mercy and compassion. God's willingness to entertain Abraham's pleas and engage in a dialogue with him suggests that divine mercy can extend to those who advocate for it. It portrays God as open to considering mercy, even in the face of judgment, and underscores His desire for justice to be balanced with compassion.

4. Human Agency and Prayer:

Abraham's intercession underscores the concept of human agency and prayer within the context of divine judgment. It implies that individuals have the capacity to influence the divine through earnest intercession. It underscores the power of prayer and advocacy on behalf of others and suggests that human actions and appeals can play a role in shaping divine outcomes.

In essence, Abraham's intercession challenges our perceptions of divine judgment, emphasizing the potential for mercy, the significance of righteousness, and the role of human agency in shaping the divine response to the moral condition of a community. It highlights the complexities of God's character, His commitment to justice, and His capacity for compassion within the Abrahamic faith traditions.

Chapter 6: The Destruction of Sodom and Gomorrah
Introduction:

The story of the destruction of Sodom and Gomorrah is a profound and impactful moment in the biblical narrative. It raises questions about divine justice, the consequences of sinful actions, and the power of intercession. To delve into this narrative is to explore themes of justice, intercession, and divine judgment.

The Sinful Cities and God's Judgment:

The cities of Sodom and Gomorrah, as portrayed in the Bible, were notorious for their wickedness and sin. Their transgressions included inhospitality, violence, and sexual immorality. Their evil ways reached a point where divine intervention became necessary.

Why God's Judgment Was Initiated:

The initiation of God's judgment was a response to the outcry against the sinful cities. Their sins had become so grave that divine intervention was required to address the moral decay and uphold divine justice.

Abraham's Plea for Mercy:

In the face of God's impending judgment, Abraham engaged in a poignant intercession. He implored God to spare the cities if righteous individuals were found within them. Abraham's plea for mercy reflects compassion, his relationship with God, and his concern for the innocent amidst the judgment.

Genesis 18:32 (ESV):

"Then he said, 'Oh let not the Lord be angry, and I will speak again but this once. Suppose ten are found there.' He answered, 'For the sake of ten, I will not destroy it.'"

This chapter delves into the profound story of the destruction of Sodom and Gomorrah, emphasizing themes of justice, intercession, and divine judgment. It explores the consequences of sinful actions and the profound impact of Abraham's plea for mercy within the patriarchal narrative, ultimately shedding light on the complexities of divine justice and the power of human advocacy in the face of divine judgment.

CHAPTER 09

SARAH AND ABIMELECH

The encounters between Abraham, Sarah, and Abimelech provide an intriguing episode in the patriarchal narrative. These interactions shed light on themes of faith, trust, and divine protection, as well as the challenges faced by the patriarchs in their journeys.

Abraham and Sarah's Encounters with Abimelech:

Abraham's journey took him to the land of Gerar, where he encountered Abimelech, the king of Gerar, on two separate occasions (Genesis 20 and 21). These encounters raise questions about the dynamics of trust and deception, as Abraham initially presented Sarah as his sister to protect himself. Abimelech unknowingly took Sarah into his harem, and God intervened to prevent her from being defiled. The subsequent interactions between Abraham, Sarah, and Abimelech illuminate the complexities of human relationships and divine protection.

The Protection of Sarah:

The narrative highlights God's protection of Sarah during her time in Abimelech's household. Through a dream, God warned Abimelech of the consequences of taking Sarah as his wife, despite her marriage to Abraham. God's intervention ensured that Sarah remained unharmed, underscoring the importance of divine providence in the lives of the patriarchs.

This chapter delves into the encounters between Abraham, Sarah, and Abimelech, emphasizing themes of trust, deception, and divine protection. It explores the complexities of human relationships and the pivotal role of God in safeguarding the matriarch, Sarah, within the patriarchal narrative.

Introduction:

The encounters between Abraham, Sarah, and Abimelech offer an intriguing episode in the patriarchal narrative. These interactions delve into themes of faith, trust, and divine protection and provide insight into the challenges faced by the patriarchs in their journeys.

What Was Going On with Sarah and Abimelech:

The episodes involving Sarah and Abimelech occurred during Abraham and Sarah's sojourn in Gerar, which was ruled by King Abimelech. Twice, Abraham presented Sarah as his sister to protect himself, leading Abimelech to take Sarah into his household, unaware that she was married to Abraham.

Abimelech:

Abimelech was the name used for the Philistine kings of Gerar in the biblical narrative. The specific Abimelech encountered by Abraham and Sarah is not necessarily the same individual each time but a title or a name used for successive Philistine kings. In this context, Abimelech was the king of Gerar during the time of Abraham and Sarah's journey.

The encounters between Abraham, Sarah, and Abimelech in Gerar raised questions about trust, deception, and divine intervention. The narrative demonstrates God's protection of Sarah and highlights the complexities of human relationships within the patriarchal narrative.

Abraham's journey to the land of Gerar brought him face to face with Abimelech, the king of that territory, during two distinct encounters, as recounted in Genesis 20 and 21. These encounters are marked by intricate dynamics of trust, deception, and divine intervention that offer valuable insights into the challenges faced by the patriarch and his wife, Sarah.

In the first encounter, detailed in Genesis 20, Abraham finds himself in Gerar and, out of fear for his own life, presents Sarah as his sister rather than his wife. This act of deception raises ethical questions about the lengths one might go to protect oneself in an unfamiliar land. Abimelech, unaware of Sarah's marital status, takes her into his harem.

The second encounter, occurring in Genesis 21, unfolds after Sarah gives birth to Isaac. Abraham and Abimelech meet to solidify a covenant, highlighting the theme of reconciliation. The tension that existed in the previous encounter is resolved through diplomacy, signifying a newfound level of trust between the two figures.

Abraham's decision to present Sarah as his sister in the first encounter raises questions about the extent to which fear and self-preservation can lead individuals to compromise their integrity. The divine intervention in both encounters serves as a reminder of God's role in protecting His chosen ones and guiding them through challenging situations.

These encounters reveal the complexities of human relationships and the moral dilemmas faced by individuals in unfamiliar territories. They also emphasize the importance of trust, truthfulness, and divine protection within the patriarchal narrative.

When Abimelech unknowingly took Sarah into his harem, and God intervened to prevent her from being defiled, it was a pivotal moment in the narrative.

In Genesis 20, God appeared to Abimelech in a dream and revealed Sarah's true identity as Abraham's wife. He warned Abimelech that taking Sarah as his wife would result in death because she was already married. Abimelech, who had acted innocently in this matter, responded by returning Sarah to Abraham, acknowledging his error, and offering gifts to Abraham.

These events illustrate the complexities of human relationships and divine protection. Abimelech's unwitting involvement with Sarah underscores the potential for misunderstandings and conflicts in human interactions. It also highlights the significance of divine intervention in ensuring the safety and integrity of individuals chosen by God.

The subsequent interactions between Abraham, Sarah, and Abimelech reflect themes of trust, diplomacy, and the need for reconciliation. The acknowledgment of the error and the exchange of gifts between Abimelech and Abraham show a desire for peaceful resolution and a renewed level of trust.

Ultimately, this episode emphasizes the importance of God's providence and protection in the lives of the patriarchs and serves as a reminder of the intricate interplay between human actions, divine intervention, and the complexities of human relationships within the patriarchal narrative.

The protection of Sarah in the narrative involving Abimelech is a testament to God's watchful care over the individuals chosen to fulfill His covenant. The significance of this protection lies in several key aspects:

1. Preservation of God's Promise: Sarah was not just Abraham's wife; she was an integral part of God's plan to fulfill His promise of making Abraham the father of many nations. God had promised that Sarah would bear a son through whom His covenant would be established. Any harm that could befall Sarah would jeopardize the fulfillment of this divine promise.

2. Divine Providence: The narrative highlights the concept of divine providence, where God actively intervenes in human affairs to ensure His will is accomplished. In this case, God's intervention through a dream served to prevent any harm from coming to Sarah and to safeguard the integrity of His plan.

3. Preservation of Moral Integrity: God's intervention also ensured the moral integrity of Sarah. She had been unknowingly placed in a situation where her marital status was misunderstood. God's protection preserved her purity and prevented her from entering into an unlawful relationship.

4. Reaffirmation of Divine Commitment: God's protection of Sarah reaffirms His commitment to His chosen people. It underscores that God is actively involved in safeguarding the lives and promises of those who are called according to His purpose.

In summary, the protection of Sarah in the encounter with Abimelech highlights God's commitment to preserving His promises and the moral integrity of His chosen ones. It underscores the importance of divine providence in the lives of the patriarchs and serves as a reminder of God's active involvement in the fulfillment of His covenant.

CHAPTER 10

THE SEARCH FOR A WIFE FOR ISAAC

The search for a wife for Isaac is a significant episode in the patriarchal narrative, reflecting Abraham's concern for his son's future and the continuation of God's covenant. This chapter explores Abraham's proactive steps to ensure Isaac's marriage aligns with God's promises and the servant's faithful journey to find a suitable wife for Isaac.

Abraham's Concern for Isaac's Marriage:

As Abraham grew older, his concern for Isaac's future became paramount. Understanding the importance of preserving the purity of their lineage and the continuation of God's covenant through Isaac, Abraham sought to find a wife for his son from his own kin, rather than from the surrounding Canaanite peoples. This decision underscored Abraham's commitment to God's plan and the preservation of his family's faith and traditions.

Genesis 24:3-4 (ESV):

"that I may make you swear by the Lord, the God of heaven and God of the earth, that you will not take a wife for my son from the daughters of the Canaanites, among whom I dwell, but will go to my country and to my kindred, and take a wife for my son Isaac."

The Servant's Journey:

Abraham entrusted his senior servant, Eliezer, with the critical task of finding a suitable wife for Isaac. Eliezer's journey to Mesopotamia, specifically to the city of Nahor, was guided by Abraham's clear instructions and the servant's reliance on God's guidance. Before setting out, Eliezer prayed for success, seeking a sign to identify the right woman for Isaac.

Genesis 24:12-14 (ESV):

"And he said, 'O Lord, God of my master Abraham, please grant me success today and show steadfast love to my master Abraham. Behold, I am standing by the spring of water, and the daughters of the men of the city are coming out to draw water. Let the young woman to whom I shall say, "Please let down your jar that I may drink," and who shall say, "Drink, and I will water your camels"—let her be the one whom you have appointed for your servant Isaac. By this I shall know that you have shown steadfast love to my master.'"

Meeting Rebekah:

Eliezer's prayers were answered when he met Rebekah at the well. She fulfilled the sign by offering water to him and his camels. Recognizing her as the woman God had chosen for Isaac, Eliezer gave her gifts and sought permission from her family for the marriage. Rebekah's family, recognizing God's hand in the matter, agreed, and Rebekah willingly chose to go with Eliezer to marry Isaac.

Genesis 24:58 (ESV):

"And they called Rebekah and said to her, 'Will you go with this man?' She said, 'I will go.'"

Rebekah's Journey to Isaac:

Rebekah's journey to meet Isaac marked the fulfillment of Abraham's hope for his son's future. Upon meeting her, Isaac took Rebekah as his wife, and she brought comfort to Isaac after the loss of his mother, Sarah. Their marriage symbolized the continuation of God's covenant and the strengthening of the patriarchal lineage.

Genesis 24:67 (ESV):

"Then Isaac brought her into the tent of Sarah his mother and took Rebekah, and she became his wife, and he loved her. So Isaac was comforted after his mother's death."

Conclusion:

The search for a wife for Isaac underscores the importance of faith, divine guidance, and the continuation of God's covenant in the patriarchal narrative. Abraham's concern for his son's marriage, the servant's faithful journey, and Rebekah's willing acceptance highlight the intricate interplay of human initiative and divine intervention in fulfilling God's promises.

CHAPTER 11

REBEKAH AND ISAAC'S MARRIAGE

The meeting and marriage of Isaac and Rebekah is a touching and significant episode in the patriarchal narrative. It highlights themes of divine providence, faith, and love, marking the continuation of God's covenant through the lineage of Abraham. This chapter explores the events leading up to their union and the establishment of their marriage.

The Meeting at the Well:

The journey to find a suitable wife for Isaac culminated in a providential encounter at a well. Abraham's servant, Eliezer, had prayed for a sign to identify the woman chosen by God for Isaac. Rebekah's actions at the well—offering water to Eliezer and his camels—fulfilled this sign, demonstrating her kindness and hospitality.

Genesis 24:17-19 (ESV):

"Then the servant ran to meet her and said, 'Please give me a little water to drink from your jar.' She said, 'Drink, my lord.' And she quickly let down her jar upon her hand and gave him a drink. When she had finished giving him a drink, she said, 'I will draw water for your camels also, until they have finished drinking.'"

Eliezer's Confirmation:

Eliezer's meeting with Rebekah at the well confirmed God's guidance in his mission. He gave her gifts of gold jewelry as tokens of betrothal and sought permission from her family for the marriage. Eliezer's account of his journey and God's intervention convinced Rebekah's family of the divine nature of the match.

Genesis 24:50-51 (ESV):

"Then Laban and Bethuel answered and said, 'The thing has come from the Lord; we cannot speak to you bad or good. Behold, Rebekah is before you, take her and go, and let her be the wife of your master's son, as the Lord has spoken.'"

Rebekah's Willingness:

Rebekah's willingness to leave her family and travel to a distant land to marry Isaac reflects her faith and readiness to embrace God's plan. Her acceptance of Eliezer's proposal and her swift departure underscore her commitment and courage.

Genesis 24:58 (ESV):

"And they called Rebekah and said to her, 'Will you go with this man?' She said, 'I will go.'"

The Marriage of Isaac and Rebekah:

Rebekah's arrival in Canaan marked the beginning of a new chapter in Isaac's life. Isaac was meditating in the field when he saw the caravan approaching. The moment they met was marked by mutual respect and affection. Isaac brought Rebekah into his mother Sarah's tent, signifying her new role as matriarch, and they became husband and wife.

Genesis 24:67 (ESV):

"Then Isaac brought her into the tent of Sarah his mother and took Rebekah, and she became his wife, and he loved her. So Isaac was comforted after his mother's death."

Conclusion:

The marriage of Isaac and Rebekah is a testament to divine providence and the continuation of God's covenant. Their union, founded on faith and guided by God's hand, ensured the perpetuation of Abraham's lineage. The story of their meeting and marriage highlights the importance of trust in God's plan and the blessings that come from obedience and faith.

CHAPTER 12

ABRAHAM'S DEATH

The death of Abraham marks the end of an era in the patriarchal narrative. As the patriarch of a great nation, his passing signifies a moment of transition for his descendants. This chapter explores the circumstances surrounding Abraham's death, the division of his inheritance, and the continuation of God's covenant through his lineage.

The Passing of the Patriarch:

Abraham lived a long and fulfilling life, reaching the age of 175 years. His life was marked by numerous encounters with God, acts of faith, and the establishment of a covenant that would define the future of his descendants. Abraham's death is recorded in Genesis 25:7-8.

Genesis 25:7-8 (ESV):

"These are the days of the years of Abraham's life, 175 years. Abraham breathed his last and died in a good old age, an old man and full of years, and was gathered to his people."

Abraham's death was peaceful, and he was described as having lived a full life. His passing was a significant moment, not just for his immediate family, but for the generations that would follow.

The Burial of Abraham:

Abraham was buried by his sons, Isaac and Ishmael, in the cave of Machpelah, which he had purchased as a burial site for Sarah. This act of unity between Isaac and Ishmael at their father's burial underscores the bond that still existed between the half-brothers despite the earlier conflicts in their family.

Genesis 25:9-10 (ESV):

"Isaac and Ishmael his sons buried him in the cave of Machpelah, in the field of Ephron the son of Zohar the Hittite, east of Mamre, the field that Abraham purchased from the Hittites. There Abraham was buried, with Sarah his wife."

The Division of His Inheritance:

Abraham's inheritance was divided among his descendants, with Isaac receiving the primary inheritance as the son of promise through whom God's covenant would continue. This included the land of Canaan and the blessings associated with God's promises.

Genesis 25:5-6 (ESV):

"Abraham gave all he had to Isaac. But to the sons of his concubines Abraham gave gifts, and while he was still living he sent them away from his son Isaac, eastward to the east country."

While Isaac received the main inheritance, Abraham also provided for his other sons, including those of his concubines, by giving them gifts and sending them to the east. This ensured that Isaac's position and the covenant promises remained intact.

The Continuation of God's Covenant:

Abraham's death did not signify the end of God's covenant but rather its continuation through Isaac. The promises made to Abraham were reaffirmed through Isaac, and the narrative transitions to the next generation, focusing on Isaac and his descendants.

Genesis 26:3-4 (ESV):

"Sojourn in this land, and I will be with you and will bless you, for to you and to your offspring I will give all these lands, and I will establish the oath that I swore to Abraham your father. I will multiply your offspring as the stars of heaven and will give to your offspring all these lands. And in your offspring, all the nations of the earth shall be blessed."

Conclusion:

The death of Abraham marks a significant transition in the patriarchal narrative. His peaceful passing, the division of his inheritance, and the continuation of God's covenant through Isaac underscore the enduring nature of God's promises. Abraham's legacy, built on faith and obedience, set the foundation for the future of his descendants and the fulfillment of God's covenantal promises.

CHAPTER 13

ISAAC'S BLESSING AND DECEPTION

The story of Isaac's blessing and the subsequent deception by Jacob and Rebekah is one of the most dramatic and complex episodes in the patriarchal narrative. It delves into themes of favoritism, deception, and the fulfillment of divine prophecy. This chapter explores the blessing of Jacob and Esau, the deception that led to the blessing of the younger son, and the consequences of these actions.

The Blessing of Jacob and Esau:

Isaac, now old and nearly blind, decided it was time to bestow his blessing upon his eldest son, Esau. In the cultural context of the time, the father's blessing was a significant event, often determining the future and fortunes of the recipient. Isaac instructed Esau to hunt game and prepare a meal for him, after which he would give him his blessing.

Genesis 27:1-4 (ESV):

"When Isaac was old and his eyes were dim so that he could not see, he called Esau his older son and said to him, 'My son'; and he answered, 'Here I am.' He said, 'Behold, I am old; I do not know the day of my death. Now then, take your weapons, your quiver, and your bow, and go out to the field and hunt game for me, and prepare for me delicious food, such as I love, and bring it to me so that I may eat, that my soul may bless you before I die.'"

The Deception by Jacob and Rebekah:

Rebekah, overhearing Isaac's plan, intervened to ensure that Jacob, her favored son, would receive the blessing instead. She devised a plan for Jacob to deceive his father by posing as Esau. Rebekah prepared a meal using goats from their flock, and she covered Jacob's hands and neck with goat skins to mimic Esau's hairy skin.

Genesis 27:15-17 (ESV):

"Then Rebekah took the best garments of Esau her older son, which were with her in the house, and put them on Jacob her younger son. And the skins of the young goats she put on his hands and on the smooth part of his neck. And she put the delicious food and the bread, which she had prepared, into the hand of her son Jacob."

Jacob, reluctant but obedient to his mother's plan, approached Isaac and successfully deceived him. Isaac, relying on touch and smell due to his blindness, was convinced that Jacob was Esau and proceeded to bless him.

Genesis 27:27-29 (ESV):

"So he came near and kissed him. And Isaac smelled the smell of his garments and blessed him and said, 'See, the smell of my son is as the smell of a field that the Lord has blessed! May God give you of the dew of heaven and of the fatness of the earth and plenty of grain and wine. Let peoples serve you, and nations bow down to you. Be lord over your brothers, and may your mother's sons bow down to you. Cursed be everyone who curses you, and blessed be everyone who blesses you!'"

The Consequences of Deception:

When Esau returned and discovered that the blessing had been given to Jacob, he was devastated and furious. He begged his father for any remaining blessing, but Isaac's primary blessing, which carried the weight of future prosperity and dominance, had already been irrevocably bestowed upon Jacob.

Genesis 27:34-36 (ESV):

"As soon as Esau heard the words of his father, he cried out with an exceedingly great and bitter cry and said to his father, 'Bless me, even me also, O my father!' But he said, 'Your brother came deceitfully, and he has taken away your blessing.' Esau said, 'Is he not rightly named Jacob? For he has cheated me these two times. He took away my birthright, and behold, now he has taken away my blessing.' Then he said, 'Have you not reserved a blessing for me?'"

Isaac, realizing the gravity of the situation, gave Esau a secondary blessing, but it did not carry the same significance as the one given to Jacob. This deception led to a deep rift between the brothers, with Esau vowing to kill Jacob once their father passed away.

Genesis 27:41 (ESV):

"Now Esau hated Jacob because of the blessing with which his father had blessed him, and Esau said to himself, 'The days of mourning for my father are approaching; then I will kill my brother Jacob.'"

Conclusion:

The story of Isaac's blessing and the deception by Jacob and Rebekah highlights the complexities of familial relationships and the fulfillment of divine prophecy, as it was foretold that the older would serve the younger (Genesis 25:23). It also underscores the consequences of deceit and favoritism within a family. This episode is a pivotal moment in the patriarchal narrative, setting the stage for Jacob's journey and the unfolding of God's plan through his descendants.

CHAPTER 14

JACOB'S JOURNEY TO HARAN

Jacob's journey to Haran marks a significant turning point in his life. Fleeing from his brother Esau's wrath, Jacob embarks on a journey to his uncle Laban's house in Haran. This chapter explores Jacob's escape, the challenges he faced on his journey, and the beginnings of his transformative experiences.

Jacob's Escape from Esau:

After deceiving his father Isaac and receiving the blessing meant for Esau, Jacob faced the fury of his brother. Esau's vow to kill Jacob forced him to leave his home in Beersheba and seek refuge with his uncle Laban in Haran.

Genesis 27:41-43 (ESV):

"Now Esau hated Jacob because of the blessing with which his father had blessed him, and Esau said to himself, 'The days of mourning for my father are approaching; then I will kill my brother Jacob.' But the words of Esau her older son were told to Rebekah. So she sent and called Jacob her younger son and said to him, 'Behold, your brother Esau comforts himself about you by planning to kill you. Now, therefore, my son, obey my voice. Arise, flee to Laban my brother in Haran.'"

The Beginning of Jacob's Journey:

Jacob's journey to Haran was both a physical and spiritual journey. As he traveled, he experienced profound moments that would shape his faith and future. One of the most significant events occurred at Bethel, where he had a dream of a ladder reaching to heaven, with angels ascending and descending on it.

Genesis 28:12-15 (ESV):

"And he dreamed, and behold, there was a ladder set up on the earth, and the top of it reached to heaven. And behold, the angels of God were ascending and descending on it! And behold, the Lord stood above it and said, 'I am the Lord, the God of Abraham your father and the God of Isaac. The land on which you lie I will give to you and to your offspring. Your offspring shall be like the dust of the earth, and you shall spread abroad to the west and to the east and to the north and to the south, and in you and your offspring shall all the families of the earth be blessed. Behold, I am with you and will keep you wherever you go, and will bring you back to this land. For I will not leave you until I have done what I have promised you.'"

Jacob's Vow at Bethel:

Awakened by this vision, Jacob recognized the place as the house of God and the gate of heaven. He set up a stone pillar and made a vow, dedicating himself to God and promising to return to this place to worship.

Genesis 28:20-22 (ESV):

"Then Jacob made a vow, saying, 'If God will be with me and will keep me in this way that I go, and will give me bread to eat and clothing to wear, so that I come again to my father's house in peace, then the Lord shall be my God, and this stone, which I have set up for a pillar, shall be God's house. And of all that you give me I will give a full tenth to you.'"

Arrival at Laban's House:

Jacob continued his journey and eventually arrived at the well near Haran, where he met Rachel, Laban's daughter. Impressed by her beauty and kindness, Jacob immediately felt a connection to her. Rachel brought Jacob to her father's house, and Laban welcomed him warmly.

Genesis 29:12-14 (ESV):

"And Jacob told Rachel that he was her father's kinsman, and that he was Rebekah's son, and she ran and told her father. As soon as Laban heard the news about Jacob, his sister's son, he ran to meet him and embraced him and kissed him and brought him to his house. Jacob told Laban all these things, and Laban said to him, 'Surely you are my bone and my flesh!' And he stayed with him a month."

Conclusion:

Jacob's journey to Haran was filled with challenges, revelations, and divine encounters. His escape from Esau's wrath and the subsequent experiences on his journey marked the beginning of his transformation. The dream at Bethel and his arrival at Laban's house set the stage for the next phase of Jacob's life, where he would face new trials, form significant relationships, and continue to grow in his faith. This chapter highlights the themes of divine guidance, personal growth, and the enduring faith that would define Jacob's journey.

CHAPTER 15

THE BIRTH OF JACOB'S SONS

The birth of Jacob's sons marks a significant chapter in the patriarchal narrative, highlighting the formation of the twelve tribes of Israel. This chapter explores Jacob's marriages to Leah and Rachel, the births of his twelve sons, and the complex family dynamics that shaped their lives.

Jacob's Marriages to Leah and Rachel:

Jacob's arrival at his uncle Laban's house set the stage for his marriage to Leah and Rachel. Jacob fell in love with Rachel, Laban's younger daughter, and agreed to work for seven years to marry her. However, Laban deceives Jacob by giving him Leah, his elder daughter, instead. Jacob then worked an additional seven years to marry Rachel.

Genesis 29:25-28 (ESV):

"And in the morning, behold, it was Leah! And Jacob said to Laban, 'What is this you have done to me? Did I not serve with you for Rachel? Why then have you deceived me?' Laban said, 'It is not so done in our country, to give the younger before the firstborn. Complete the week of this one, and we will give you the other also in return for serving me another seven years.' Jacob did so, and completed her week. Then Laban gave him his daughter Rachel to be his wife."

The Birth of Jacob's Sons:

Jacob's family grew rapidly, with the birth of twelve sons from his marriages to Leah, Rachel, and their maidservants, Zilpah and Bilhah. The sons' births are detailed as follows:

1. Leah's Sons: Leah gave birth to six sons—Reuben, Simeon, Levi, Judah, Issachar, and Zebulun. She also had a daughter, Dinah.

2. Bilhah's Sons: Rachel's maidservant, Bilhah, gave birth to two sons—Dan and Naphtali.

3. Zilpah's Sons: Leah's maidservant, Zilpah, gave birth to two sons—Gad and Asher.

4. Rachel's Sons: Rachel, who was initially barren, eventually gave birth to two sons—Joseph and Benjamin.

Genesis 29:31-35; 30:1-24 (ESV) provides the detailed accounts of these births.

Reuben:

"Leah conceived and bore a son, and she called his name Reuben, for she said, 'Because the Lord has looked upon my affliction; for now my husband will love me.'"

Simeon:

"She conceived again and bore a son, and said, 'Because the Lord has heard that I am hated, he has given me this son also.' And she called his name Simeon."

Levi:

"Again she conceived and bore a son, and said, 'Now this time my husband will be attached to me, because I have borne him three sons.' Therefore his name was called Levi."

Judah:

"And she conceived again and bore a son, and said, 'This time I will praise the Lord.' Therefore she called his name Judah. Then she ceased bearing."

Dan:

"Rachel said, 'God has judged me, and has also heard my voice and given me a son.' Therefore she called his name Dan."

Naphtali:

"Rachel said, 'With mighty wrestlings I have wrestled with my sister and have prevailed.' So she called his name Naphtali."

Gad:

"Leah said, 'Good fortune has come!' so she called his name Gad."

Asher:

"Leah said, 'Happy am I! For women have called me happy.' So she called his name Asher."

Issachar:

"Leah said, 'God has given me my wages because I gave my servant to my husband.' So she called his name Issachar."

Zebulun:

"Leah said, 'God has endowed me with a good endowment; now my husband will honor me, because I have borne him six sons.' So she called his name Zebulun."

Joseph:

"God remembered Rachel, and God listened to her and opened her womb. She conceived and bore a son and said, 'God has taken away my reproach.' And she called his name Joseph, saying, 'May the Lord add to me another son!'"

Benjamin:

Rachel later gave birth to Benjamin, but she died during childbirth.

Genesis 35:16-19 (ESV):

"Then they journeyed from Bethel. When they were still some distance from Ephrath, Rachel went into labor, and she had hard labor. And when her labor was at its hardest, the midwife said to her, 'Do not fear, for you have another son.' And as her soul was departing (for she was dying), she called his name Ben-oni; but his father called him Benjamin. So Rachel died, and she was buried on the way to Ephrath (that is, Bethlehem)."

Complex Family Dynamics:

The births of Jacob's twelve sons brought about complex family dynamics, marked by jealousy, competition, and favoritism. Rachel's favored status and her initial barrenness created tension between her and Leah. The use of maidservants as surrogates further complicated relationships within the family. These dynamics set the stage for future conflicts and the unfolding of God's plan through Jacob's descendants.

Conclusion:

The birth of Jacob's twelve sons is a pivotal event in the patriarchal narrative, establishing the foundations of the twelve tribes of Israel. Jacob's marriages to Leah and Rachel, along with the involvement of Zilpah and Bilhah, highlight the complexities of family life and the fulfillment of God's promises. This chapter underscores the themes of divine providence, human frailty, and the unfolding of God's plan through the lineage of Jacob.

CHAPTER 16

THE RETURN OF JACOB

The return of Jacob to Canaan is a pivotal moment in the patriarchal narrative, marked by his reconciliation with Esau and the fulfillment of God's promise to bring him back to the land of his fathers. This chapter explores the journey of reconciliation between Jacob and Esau and Jacob's return to Canaan, highlighting themes of forgiveness, divine guidance, and the continuation of God's covenant.

Jacob's Reconciliation with Esau:

Jacob's departure from Laban's household was prompted by a divine command to return to his homeland. However, the prospect of facing Esau, whom he had deceived and whose birthright he had taken, was daunting. Jacob prepared for the encounter with great trepidation, sending messengers ahead with gifts to appease Esau.

Genesis 32:3-5 (ESV):

"And Jacob sent messengers before him to Esau his brother in the land of Seir, the country of Edom, instructing them, 'Thus you shall say to my lord Esau: Thus says your servant Jacob, "I have sojourned with Laban and stayed until now. I have oxen, donkeys, flocks, male servants, and female servants. I have sent to tell my lord, so that I may find favor in your sight."'"

Before meeting Esau, Jacob had a profound spiritual encounter at Peniel, where he wrestled with a divine being. This struggle left Jacob with a limp but also a new name, Israel, symbolizing his perseverance and transformation.

Genesis 32:28-30 (ESV):

"Then he said, 'Your name shall no longer be called Jacob, but Israel, for you have striven with God and with men, and have prevailed.' Then Jacob asked him, 'Please tell me your name.' But he said, 'Why is it that you ask my name?' And there he blessed him. So Jacob called the name of the place Peniel, saying, 'For I have seen God face to face, and yet my life has been delivered.'"

When Jacob finally met Esau, the anticipated confrontation turned into a moving scene of reconciliation.

Esau ran to meet Jacob, embracing him and weeping. This act of forgiveness marked a significant turning point in their relationship.

Genesis 33:4 (ESV):

"But Esau ran to meet him and embraced him and fell on his neck and kissed him, and they wept."

Jacob's heartfelt gesture of presenting gifts and bowing to Esau further demonstrated his humility and desire for reconciliation. Esau's acceptance of the gifts and their subsequent dialogue reflected a mutual willingness to mend their relationship.

Genesis 33:10-11 (ESV):

"Jacob said, 'No, please, if I have found favor in your sight, then accept my present from my hand. For I have seen your face, which is like seeing the face of God, and you have accepted me. Please accept my blessing that is brought to you, because God has dealt graciously with me, and because I have enough.' Thus he urged him, and he took it."

Jacob's Return to Canaan:

Following the reconciliation with Esau, Jacob continued his journey back to Canaan, settling in Shechem and later in Bethel, where God reaffirmed His covenant with Jacob.

Genesis 35:1 (ESV):

"God said to Jacob, 'Arise, go up to Bethel and dwell there. Make an altar there to the God who appeared to you when you fled from your brother Esau.'"

At Bethel, God reiterated the promises He had made to Abraham and Isaac, emphasizing that Jacob's descendants would inherit the land and become a great nation.

Genesis 35:9-12 (ESV):

"God appeared to Jacob again, when he came from Paddan-aram, and blessed him. And God said to him, 'Your name is Jacob; no longer shall your name be called Jacob, but Israel shall be your name.' So he called his name Israel. And God said to him, 'I am God Almighty: be fruitful and multiply. A nation and a company of nations shall come from you, and kings shall come from your own body. The land that I gave to Abraham and Isaac I will give to you, and I will give the land to your offspring after you.'"

The Burial of Isaac:

Jacob's return to Canaan also involved the burial of his father, Isaac. Together with Esau, they buried Isaac in the family tomb at Machpelah, signifying a moment of unity and respect for their shared heritage.

Genesis 35:29 (ESV):

"And Isaac breathed his last, and he died and was gathered to his people, old and full of days. And his sons Esau and Jacob buried him."

Conclusion:

Jacob's return to Canaan and his reconciliation with Esau highlight themes of forgiveness, divine guidance, and the fulfillment of God's promises. The journey underscores the transformative power of reconciliation and the importance of faith in overcoming past wrongs. Jacob's return and the reaffirmation of God's covenant mark a continuation of the patriarchal narrative, ensuring the legacy of Abraham through the lineage of Jacob, now called Israel.

CHAPTER 17

THE DEATH OF ISAAC

The death of Isaac marks the end of another significant era in the patriarchal narrative. As the son of Abraham and the father of Jacob and Esau, Isaac's life and legacy are pivotal in the continuation of God's covenant with His chosen people. This chapter explores the circumstances surrounding Isaac's passing and the legacy he leaves behind.

The Passing of Isaac:

Isaac lived a long and fruitful life, reaching the age of 180 years. His passing is noted with respect and reverence, highlighting his importance in the lineage of the patriarchs.

Genesis 35:28-29 (ESV):

"Now the days of Isaac were 180 years. And Isaac breathed his last, and he died and was gathered to his people, old and full of days. And his sons Esau and Jacob buried him."

Isaac's death was peaceful, and he was described as having lived to a "good old age." His sons, Esau and Jacob, despite their previous conflicts, came together to bury their father. This act of unity underscores the respect and honor they held for Isaac and serves as a moment of reconciliation between the brothers.

The Burial of Isaac:

Isaac was buried in the family tomb at Machpelah, the same burial site as his father Abraham and his wife Sarah. This burial site, purchased by Abraham, held significant importance as the family's resting place, symbolizing their lasting presence in the Promised Land.

Genesis 49:31 (ESV):

"There they buried Abraham and Sarah his wife. There they buried Isaac and Rebekah his wife, and there I buried Leah."

The Legacy of Isaac:

Isaac's legacy is multifaceted, encompassing his role as a patriarch, his contributions to the continuity of God's covenant, and his influence on his sons, Jacob and Esau.

1. Patriarchal Role: Isaac's life continued the lineage and the covenant established by God with Abraham. His faith and obedience to God's commands reinforced the patriarchal foundation and set an example for future generations.

2. Faith and Obedience: Isaac's willingness to follow God's will, from his near-sacrifice on Mount Moriah to his blessings upon Jacob and Esau, demonstrates his deep faith and trust in God's plan. His life is a testament to the importance of obedience and faithfulness.

3. Fatherhood and Blessings: As the father of Jacob and Esau, Isaac's blessings and the subsequent fulfillment of those blessings played a crucial role in the unfolding of the biblical narrative. Despite the deception involved in Jacob receiving the blessing meant for Esau, Isaac's actions were integral to the continuation of God's plan for His people.

4. Symbol of Continuity: Isaac's life and actions symbolized the continuity of God's promises. Through Isaac, the covenant was passed down to Jacob, ensuring that the lineage of Abraham would continue and that the promises of land, descendants, and blessing would be fulfilled.

Conclusion:

The death of Isaac marks a significant transition in the patriarchal narrative. His peaceful passing and burial, attended by both of his sons, symbolize unity and respect. Isaac's legacy as a patriarch, his faith and obedience, and his role in the continuation of God's covenant leave a lasting impact on the history of the Israelites. As the torch of God's promises passes to the next generation, Isaac's life serves as a testament to the enduring faith and commitment required to fulfill God's plan.

CHAPTER 18

JACOB'S ENCOUNTER WITH GOD

Jacob's encounter with God at Peniel is one of the most profound and transformative moments in the patriarchal narrative. This chapter delves into the dramatic wrestling match between Jacob and a divine being, the significance of this encounter, and Jacob's subsequent name change to Israel. This event highlights themes of struggle, transformation, and the reaffirmation of God's covenant.

Jacob's Wrestling with God at Peniel:

As Jacob was returning to Canaan with his family and possessions, he was filled with apprehension about meeting his brother Esau, whom he had wronged many years earlier. Seeking solace and strength, Jacob sent his family and possessions across the Jabbok River and spent the night alone. It was during this solitary time that Jacob encountered a mysterious figure, later revealed to be a divine being, and engaged in a physical struggle that lasted until dawn.

Genesis 32:24-26 (ESV):

"And Jacob was left alone. And a man wrestled with him until the breaking of the day. When the man saw that he did not prevail against Jacob, he touched his hip socket, and Jacob's hip was put out of joint as he wrestled with him. Then he said, 'Let me go, for the day has broken.' But Jacob said, 'I will not let you go unless you bless me.'"

This wrestling match symbolizes Jacob's intense spiritual and emotional struggle. Despite the pain and exhaustion, Jacob's determination to seek a blessing reflects his deep desire for God's favor and assurance.

The Significance of the Encounter:

The encounter at Peniel is significant for several reasons. First, it represents a turning point in Jacob's life, where he confronts his past actions, fears, and doubts. The physical struggle mirrors his inner turmoil and his quest for a new identity and purpose.

Genesis 32:27-28 (ESV):

"And he said to him, 'What is your name?' And he said, 'Jacob.' Then he said, 'Your name shall no longer be called

Jacob, but Israel, for you have striven with God and with men, and have prevailed.'"

Jacob's Name Change to Israel:

In recognition of his perseverance and determination, the divine being blesses Jacob and changes his name to Israel, meaning "he who strives with God" or "God contends." This name change signifies Jacob's transformation and his new role as the patriarch of a great nation.

Genesis 32:29-30 (ESV):

"Then Jacob asked him, 'Please tell me your name.' But he said, 'Why is it that you ask my name?' And there he blessed him. So Jacob called the name of the place Peniel, saying, 'For I have seen God face to face, and yet my life has been delivered.'"

The new name, Israel, marks a significant shift in Jacob's identity. No longer defined solely by his past actions and deceit, Jacob is now recognized for his strength and perseverance in seeking God's blessing. This transformation sets the stage for the continuation of God's covenant through his descendants.

The Aftermath and Reaffirmation:

Jacob's encounter with God left him with a lasting physical reminder of the struggle—his limp, caused by the displacement of his hip. This physical change serves as a symbol of his transformed identity and the profound impact of his divine encounter.

Genesis 32:31-32 (ESV):

"The sun rose upon him as he passed Penuel, limping because of his hip. Therefore to this day the people of Israel do not eat the sinew of the thigh that is on the hip socket, because he touched the socket of Jacob's hip on the sinew of the thigh."

Following this encounter, Jacob's relationship with God is reaffirmed, and he moves forward with renewed faith and confidence. His new name, Israel, becomes the name of the nation that will descend from him, signifying the enduring nature of God's covenant and the ongoing story of God's chosen people.

Conclusion:

Jacob's encounter with God at Peniel is a defining moment in the patriarchal narrative. The wrestling match symbolizes Jacob's struggle with his past, his determination to seek God's blessing, and his transformation into Israel. This event underscores themes of struggle, perseverance, and divine favor, highlighting the continued fulfillment of God's covenant through Jacob and his descendants. The new name, Israel, marks the beginning of a new chapter in the story of God's chosen people and their journey of faith.

CHAPTER 19

JOSEPH'S STORY

The story of Joseph, one of the most captivating and detailed narratives in the Bible, begins with a focus on his relationship with his father Jacob and his brothers. This chapter explores Joseph's special coat, his prophetic dreams, and the intense jealousy these blessings evoke in his brothers, setting the stage for the dramatic events that follow.

The Special Coat:

Joseph was the eleventh son of Jacob and the firstborn of Rachel, Jacob's beloved wife. Jacob's deep affection for Joseph was evident in the special coat he made for him, often referred to as the "coat of many colors." This coat was a symbol of Jacob's favoritism, which did not go unnoticed by his other sons.

Genesis 37:3 (ESV):

"Now Israel loved Joseph more than any other of his sons, because he was the son of his old age. And he made him a robe of many colors."

The coat not only represented Jacob's love but also indicated a position of honor and authority within the family, which further fueled his brothers' resentment.

Joseph's Dreams:

Joseph's story took a significant turn when he began to have prophetic dreams. These dreams, which he eagerly shared with his family, hinted at a future where he would rise to a position of great prominence and his family members would bow down to him. This prophecy did not sit well with his brothers, already envious of their father's favoritism.

Genesis 37:5-8 (ESV):

"Now Joseph had a dream, and when he told it to his brothers they hated him even more. He said to them, 'Hear this dream that I have dreamed: Behold, we were binding sheaves in the field, and behold, my sheaf arose and stood upright. And behold, your sheaves gathered around it and bowed down to my sheaf.' His brothers said to him, 'Are you indeed to reign over us? Or are you indeed to rule over us?'

So they hated him even more for his dreams and for his words."

In another dream, Joseph saw the sun, the moon, and eleven stars bowing down to him, which he also shared with his family, including his father Jacob.

Genesis 37:9-11 (ESV):

"Then he dreamed another dream and told it to his brothers and said, 'Behold, I have dreamed another dream. Behold, the sun, the moon, and eleven stars were bowing down to me.' But when he told it to his father and to his brothers, his father rebuked him and said to him, 'What is this dream that you have dreamed? Shall I and your mother and your brothers indeed come to bow ourselves to the ground before you?' And his brothers were jealous of him, but his father kept the saying in mind."

His Brothers' Jealousy:

The combination of Jacob's blatant favoritism and Joseph's dreams of future dominance created a toxic atmosphere among the brothers. Their jealousy and hatred toward Joseph grew to dangerous levels, leading them to conspire against him.

Genesis 37:18-20 (ESV):

"They saw him from afar, and before he came near to them they conspired against him to kill him. They said to one another, 'Here comes this dreamer. Come now, let us kill him and throw him into one of the pits. Then we will say that a fierce animal has devoured him, and we will see what will become of his dreams.'"

The brothers' initial plan was to kill Joseph, but Reuben, the eldest, intervened, suggesting they throw him into a pit instead, hoping to rescue him later. This plan set in motion a series of events that would dramatically alter Joseph's life and the future of their family.

Genesis 37:21-24 (ESV):

"But when Reuben heard it, he rescued him out of their hands, saying, 'Let us not take his life.' And Reuben said to them, 'Shed no blood; throw him into this pit here in the wilderness, but do not lay a hand on him'—that he might rescue him out of their hand to restore him to his father. So when Joseph came to his brothers, they stripped him of his robe, the robe of many colors that he wore. And they took him and threw him into a pit. The pit was empty; there was no water in it."

Conclusion:

The beginning of Joseph's story is marked by favoritism, dreams of greatness, and intense sibling rivalry. The special coat and the prophetic dreams highlight Joseph's unique position and the potential for future greatness, while his brothers' jealousy sets the stage for dramatic conflict. This chapter lays the groundwork for the unfolding saga of Joseph's trials, resilience, and ultimate rise to power, illustrating the themes of divine providence, faith, and redemption that run throughout his story.

CHAPTER 20

JOSEPH'S BETRAYAL AND JOURNEY TO EGYPT

Joseph's story takes a dramatic turn with his betrayal by his brothers and his subsequent journey to Egypt. This chapter explores the pivotal events of Joseph being sold into slavery and his remarkable rise to prominence in Egypt, highlighting themes of resilience, divine providence, and redemption.

The Selling of Joseph into Slavery:

Joseph's brothers, consumed by jealousy and anger over their father's favoritism and Joseph's prophetic dreams, conspired to get rid of him. Initially planning to kill him, they ultimately decided to sell him into slavery.

Genesis 37:26-28 (ESV):

"Then Judah said to his brothers, 'What profit is it if we kill our brother and conceal his blood? Come, let us sell him to the Ishmaelites, and let not our hand be upon him, for he is our brother, our flesh.' And his brothers listened to him. Then Midianite traders passed by. And they drew Joseph up and lifted him out of the pit, and sold him to the Ishmaelites for twenty shekels of silver. They took Joseph to Egypt."

This act of betrayal by his flesh and blood marked the beginning of Joseph's long and arduous journey away from his home and into the unknown land of Egypt.

Joseph in Potiphar's House:

Upon arriving in Egypt, Joseph was sold to Potiphar, an officer of Pharaoh and the captain of the guard. Despite his dire circumstances, Joseph's unwavering faith and integrity set him apart. God was with Joseph, blessing everything he did and granting him favor in Potiphar's eyes.

Genesis 39:2-4 (ESV):

"The Lord was with Joseph, and he became a successful man, and he was in the house of his Egyptian master. His master saw that the Lord was with him and that the Lord caused all that he did to succeed in his hands. So Joseph found favor in his sight and attended him, and he made him overseer of his house and put him in charge of all that he had."

Joseph's diligent work and divine favor led to his rise within Potiphar's household, where he was entrusted with significant responsibilities. However, this period of relative stability was soon disrupted by false accusations.

False Accusations and Imprisonment:

Potiphar's wife, attracted to Joseph, attempted to seduce him. When Joseph refused her advances, she falsely accused him of attempting to assault her. Potiphar, believing his wife's claims, had Joseph thrown into prison.

Genesis 39:19-20 (ESV):

"As soon as his master heard the words that his wife spoke to him, 'This is the way your servant treated me,' his anger was kindled. And Joseph's master took him and put him into the prison, the place where the king's prisoners were confined, and he was there in prison."

Despite the unjust imprisonment, Joseph's faith remained steadfast. Even in prison, God's favor continued to follow him.

Joseph's Rise in Prison:

In prison, Joseph's leadership qualities and divine favor were again evident. The prison warden recognized his abilities and entrusted him with the care of other prisoners.

Genesis 39:21-23 (ESV):

"But the Lord was with Joseph and showed him steadfast love and gave him favor in the sight of the keeper of the prison. And the keeper of the prison put Joseph in charge of all the prisoners who were in the prison. Whatever was done there, he was the one who did it. The keeper of the prison paid no attention to anything that was in Joseph's charge, because the Lord was with him. And whatever he did, the Lord made it succeed."

While in prison, Joseph interpreted the dreams of Pharaoh's chief cupbearer and chief baker, both of whom were also imprisoned. His accurate interpretations of their dreams eventually led to a significant opportunity.

Pharaoh's Dreams and Joseph's Rise to Power:

Two years after interpreting the dreams of the cupbearer and baker, Pharaoh himself had troubling dreams that none of his advisors could interpret. The cupbearer remembered Joseph and mentioned his ability to interpret dreams to Pharaoh. Joseph was summoned from prison to interpret Pharaoh's dreams.

Genesis 41:14-16 (ESV):

"Then Pharaoh sent and called Joseph, and they quickly brought him out of the pit. And when he had shaved himself and changed his clothes, he came in before Pharaoh. And Pharaoh said to Joseph, 'I have had a dream, and there is no one who can interpret it. I have heard it said of you that when you hear a dream you can interpret it.' Joseph answered Pharaoh, 'It is not in me; God will give Pharaoh a favorable answer.'"

Joseph interpreted Pharaoh's dreams as a warning of seven years of plenty followed by seven years of severe famine. He advised Pharaoh to store surplus grain during the years of plenty to prepare for the famine. Impressed by Joseph's wisdom, Pharaoh appointed him as the second-in-command in Egypt, responsible for implementing this plan.

Genesis 41:39-41 (ESV):

"Then Pharaoh said to Joseph, 'Since God has shown you all this, there is none so discerning and wise as you are. You shall be over my house, and all my people shall order themselves as you command. Only as regards the throne will I be greater than you.' And Pharaoh said to Joseph, 'See, I have set you over all the land of Egypt.'"

Conclusion:

Joseph's journey from betrayal and slavery to imprisonment and eventual rise to power in Egypt is a testament to his resilience, faith, and God's providence. Despite the many hardships he faced, Joseph remained steadfast and trusted in God's plan. His rise to prominence in Egypt set the stage for the fulfillment of God's promises and the preservation of his family during the impending famine. This chapter highlights themes of perseverance, divine intervention, and redemption, illustrating the profound ways in which God can work through the most challenging circumstances to fulfill His purposes.

CHAPTER 21

THE REUNION OF JOSEPH AND HIS BROTHERS

The reunion of Joseph and his brothers is one of the most emotionally charged and significant moments in the biblical narrative. This chapter explores the events leading up to this dramatic reunion, focusing on the famine in Canaan, the brothers' trip to Egypt, and the powerful revelation of Joseph's true identity. Themes of forgiveness, divine providence, and family reconciliation are central to this chapter.

The Famine in Canaan:

The famine that Joseph had predicted through Pharaoh's dreams extended far beyond Egypt, affecting surrounding regions, including Canaan, where Jacob and his family resided. As the famine worsened, Jacob learned that there was grain available in Egypt and sent his sons to buy food.

Genesis 42:1-2 (ESV):

"When Jacob learned that there was grain for sale in Egypt, he said to his sons, 'Why do you look at one another?' And he said, 'Behold, I have heard that there is grain for sale in Egypt. Go down and buy grain for us there, that we may live and not die.'"

The Brothers' Trip to Egypt:

Ten of Jacob's sons traveled to Egypt to buy grain, leaving Benjamin, the youngest, behind with their father. Upon arriving in Egypt, they were brought before Joseph, who was now the governor and in charge of selling grain. Although they did not recognize Joseph, he immediately recognized them and remembered his dreams.

Genesis 42:6-8 (ESV):

"Now Joseph was governor over the land. He was the one who sold to all the people of the land. And Joseph's brothers came and bowed themselves before him with their faces to the ground. Joseph saw his brothers and recognized them, but he treated them like strangers and spoke roughly to them. 'Where do you come from?' he said. They said, 'From the land of Canaan, to buy food.' And Joseph recognized his brothers, but they did not recognize him."

Joseph's Testing of His Brothers:

Joseph decided to test his brothers to see if they had changed since the time they had sold him into slavery. He accused them of being spies and imprisoned them for three days. On the third day, he proposed a test: one brother would remain in Egypt while the others returned to Canaan with grain and brought back their youngest brother, Benjamin, to prove their honesty.

Genesis 42:18-20 (ESV):

"On the third day Joseph said to them, 'Do this and you will live, for I fear God: if you are honest men, let one of your brothers remain confined where you are in custody, and let the rest go and carry grain for the famine of your households, and bring your youngest brother to me. So your words will be verified, and you shall not die.' And they did so."

Simeon was chosen to stay behind while the rest returned to Canaan. The brothers were distressed, believing their misfortune was a result of their past sins against Joseph. Upon returning home, they informed Jacob of the governor's demands, but Jacob was initially reluctant to send Benjamin.

Genesis 42:36 (ESV):

"And Jacob their father said to them, 'You have bereaved me of my children: Joseph is no more, and Simeon is no more, and now you would take Benjamin. All this has come against me.'"

The Second Trip to Egypt:

As the famine persisted, Jacob eventually agreed to send Benjamin with his brothers to Egypt, along with gifts and double the money for the grain. Judah promised to take personal responsibility for Benjamin's safety.

Genesis 43:8-9 (ESV):

"And Judah said to Israel his father, 'Send the boy with me, and we will arise and go, that we may live and not die, both we and you and also our little ones. I will be a pledge of his safety. From my hand you shall require him. If I do not bring him back to you and set him before you, then let me bear the blame forever.'"

Upon their return to Egypt, Joseph invited them to his house for a meal. During the meal, he continued to test them, seating them according to their birth order and giving Benjamin five times as much food as the others. This favoritism was a deliberate test to see if they had changed their attitude toward their younger brother.

Genesis 43:33-34 (ESV):

"And they sat before him, the firstborn according to his birthright and the youngest according to his youth. And the men looked at one another in amazement. Portions were taken to them from Joseph's table, but Benjamin's portion was five times as much as any of theirs. And they drank and were merry with him."

The Final Test and Revelation:

Joseph's final test involved planting his silver cup in Benjamin's sack and accusing the brothers of theft. When the cup was discovered, the brothers were brought back to Joseph. Judah pleaded for Benjamin's release, offering himself as a substitute, demonstrating a profound change in his character and concern for his father and brother.

Genesis 44:33-34 (ESV):

"Now therefore, please let your servant remain instead of the boy as a servant to my lord, and let the boy go back with his brothers. For how can I go back to my father if the boy is not with me? I fear to see the evil that would find my father."

Moved by Judah's plea and the evident transformation in his brothers, Joseph could no longer contain his emotions. He revealed his true identity to them, leading to a moment of profound reconciliation.

Genesis 45:1-3 (ESV):

"Then Joseph could not control himself before all those who stood by him. He cried, 'Make everyone go out from me.' So no one stayed with him when Joseph made himself known to his brothers. And he wept aloud, so that the

Egyptians heard it, and the household of Pharaoh heard it. And Joseph said to his brothers, 'I am Joseph! Is my father still alive?' But his brothers could not answer him, for they were dismayed at his presence."

The Revelation of Joseph's True Identity:

Joseph's revelation to his brothers was a moment of shock and relief. He reassured them, expressing forgiveness and understanding that his journey to Egypt was part of God's greater plan to save their family from the famine.

Genesis 45:4-8 (ESV):

"So Joseph said to his brothers, 'Come near to me, please.' And they came near. And he said, 'I am your brother, Joseph, whom you sold into Egypt. And now do not be distressed or angry with yourselves because you sold me here, for God sent me before you to preserve life. For the famine has been in the land these two years, and there are yet five years in which there will be neither plowing nor harvest. And God sent me before you to preserve for you a remnant on earth, and to keep alive for you many survivors. So it was not you who sent me here, but God. He has made me a father to Pharaoh, and lord of all his house and ruler over all the land of Egypt.'"

Joseph's forgiveness and recognition of God's providence exemplify the themes of reconciliation and divine purpose. He instructed his brothers to bring their father and families to Egypt, where they would be provided for during the remaining years of famine.

Genesis 45:9-11 (ESV):

"Hurry and go up to my father and say to him, 'Thus says your son Joseph, God has made me lord of all Egypt. Come down to me; do not tarry. You shall dwell in the land of Goshen, and you shall be near me, you and your children and your children's children, and your flocks, your herds, and all that you have. There I will provide for you, for there are yet five years of famine to come, so that you and your household, and all that you have, do not come to poverty.'"

Conclusion:

The reunion of Joseph and his brothers is a powerful story of forgiveness, divine providence, and family reconciliation. The famine in Canaan and the brothers' trips to Egypt set the stage for the dramatic revelation of Joseph's true identity. Through these events, the narrative illustrates the transformative power of forgiveness and the unfolding of God's plan through human actions. The reunion not only restores familial bonds but also ensures the survival and prosperity of Jacob's family, fulfilling God's covenant promises.

CHAPTER 22

THE LEGACY OF ABRAHAM, ISHMAEL, AND ISAAC

The lives and legacies of Abraham, Ishmael, and Isaac are foundational to the history of the Israelites and have profound implications for the world's religious and cultural heritage. This chapter reflects on the enduring impact of these patriarchs, examining their contributions to the development of faith, their roles in shaping the Israelite nation, and their significance in the broader context of world history.

Abraham: The Father of Many Nations

Abraham is revered as the patriarch of monotheistic faiths, including Judaism, Christianity, and Islam. His unwavering faith, obedience to God's commands, and the covenant established with him form the cornerstone of his legacy. Abraham's journey from Ur to Canaan, his willingness to sacrifice Isaac, and his life of faithfulness are celebrated as exemplars of trust in God's promises.

Genesis 17:4-5 (ESV):

"Behold, my covenant is with you, and you shall be the father of a multitude of nations. No longer shall your name be called Abram, but your name shall be Abraham, for I have made you the father of a multitude of nations."

Abraham's legacy is not confined to his immediate descendants but extends to all who embrace the faith traditions that trace their origins to him. His story symbolizes the beginning of a divine relationship with humanity, emphasizing faith, obedience, and the fulfillment of God's promises.

Ishmael: The Father of a Great Nation

Ishmael, Abraham's firstborn son through Hagar, also holds a significant place in the biblical narrative and in the history of the Arab peoples. Although not the child of the covenant through whom the Israelite lineage would continue, Ishmael was blessed by God to become a great nation.

Genesis 21:13 (ESV):

"And I will make a nation of the son of the slave woman also because he is your offspring."

Ishmael's descendants are traditionally considered the ancestors of many Arab tribes. His story highlights themes of God's compassion and provision, as well as the complexity of human relationships within the framework of divine promises. Ishmael's legacy is particularly significant in Islamic tradition, where he is regarded as a prophet and an ancestor of Muhammad.

Isaac: The Child of Promise

Isaac, the child of promise born to Abraham and Sarah, represents the continuation of God's covenant with Abraham. His life is marked by faith and obedience, mirroring his father's qualities. The near-sacrifice of Isaac on Mount Moriah is a pivotal moment, demonstrating his submission to God's will and prefiguring later theological themes in Christianity.

Genesis 26:4 (ESV):

"I will multiply your offspring as the stars of heaven and will give to your offspring all these lands. And in your offspring, all the nations of the earth shall be blessed."

Isaac's role as the father of Jacob and Esau ensures the continuation of the covenantal line, leading to the establishment of the twelve tribes of Israel through Jacob. Isaac's legacy is integral to the identity and history of the Israelite nation.

The Impact on the Israelites:

The legacies of Abraham, Ishmael, and Isaac are intricately woven into the fabric of Israelite history. Abraham's covenant with God laid the foundation for the Israelite identity and their relationship with God. Isaac's lineage continued this covenant, leading to the formation of the twelve tribes of Israel. Even Ishmael's story, though separate, influenced the broader narrative of the region's peoples and their interactions with the Israelites.

The patriarchal narratives provide a theological and moral framework for the Israelite people, emphasizing themes of faith, obedience, and divine providence. The promises made to Abraham and Isaac about land, descendants, and blessings became central to the Israelite identity and their understanding of God's plans for them.

The Broader World Impact:

The influence of Abraham, Ishmael, and Isaac extends beyond the confines of Israelite history, impacting the religious and cultural development of a significant portion of the world's population. In Judaism, Abraham is the father of the Jewish nation, Isaac is a pivotal figure, and the promises to these patriarchs shape Jewish identity and faith.

In Christianity, Abraham's faith is seen as a precursor to the faith required in Jesus Christ, and Isaac's near-sacrifice is viewed as a foreshadowing of Jesus' crucifixion. The New

Testament often references these patriarchs to illustrate the continuity of God's plan.

In Islam, Abraham (Ibrahim) and Ishmael (Ismail) are central figures. Abraham's faith and obedience are celebrated, and Ishmael is considered a prophet and ancestor of Muhammad. The annual Hajj pilgrimage includes rituals that commemorate Abraham and Ishmael's faith and actions.

Conclusion:

The legacies of Abraham, Ishmael, and Isaac are enduring and far-reaching, influencing religious beliefs, cultural identities, and historical narratives across the globe. Their lives and stories are foundational to Judaism, Christianity, and Islam, and their impact continues to be felt in the faith and practices of billions of people today. Reflecting on their contributions and the themes of faith, obedience, and divine promise that characterize their stories, we see the profound ways in which these patriarchs have shaped the course of history and the spiritual heritage of humanity.

BIBLIOGRAPHY

The Holy Bible, English Standard Version. Crossway, 2001.

Alter, Robert. The Five Books of Moses: A Translation with Commentary. W. W. Norton & Company, 2004.

Hamilton, Victor P. The Book of Genesis, Chapters 1-17. Eerdmans, 1990.

Hamilton, Victor P. The Book of Genesis, Chapters 18-50. Eerdmans, 1995.

Kidner, Derek. Genesis: An Introduction and Commentary. Inter-Varsity Press, 1967.

Sarna, Nahum M. Understanding Genesis: The Heritage of Biblical Israel. Schocken Books, 1970.

Speiser, E. A. Genesis: Introduction, Translation, and Notes. Anchor Bible Series, Doubleday, 1964.

Walton, John H. The NIV Application Commentary: Genesis. Zondervan, 2001.

Wenham, Gordon J. Genesis 1-15, Volume 1 (Word Biblical Commentary). Zondervan, 1987.

Wenham, Gordon J. Genesis 16-50, Volume 2 (Word Biblical Commentary). Zondervan, 1994.

Westermann, Claus. Genesis 12-36: A Commentary. Fortress Press, 1985.

Westermann, Claus. Genesis 37-50: A Commentary. Fortress Press, 1986.

Ancient Near Eastern Texts Relating to the Old Testament, edited by James B. Pritchard. Princeton University Press, 1969.

Coogan, Michael D., editor. The Oxford History of the Biblical World. Oxford University Press, 1998.

Dever, William G. Who Were the Early Israelites and Where Did They Come From? Eerdmans, 2003.

Finkelstein, Israel, and Neil Asher Silberman. The Bible Unearthed: Archaeology's New Vision of Ancient Israel and the Origin of Its Sacred Texts. Free Press, 2001.

Fretheim, Terence E. Abraham: Trials of Family and Faith. University of South Carolina Press, 2007.

Matthews, Victor H. The Cultural World of the Bible: An Illustrated Guide to Manners and Customs. Baker Academic, 2006.

Mendenhall, George E., and Gary A. Herion. "Covenant." Anchor Bible Dictionary. Doubleday, 1992.

Soggin, J. Alberto. Introduction to the Old Testament. Westminster John Knox Press, 1989.